Gift of the Suitcase

Gift of the Suitcase

A Memoir

Ruth Glover

© 2016 by Ruth Glover. All rights reserved. No part of this book may be used or reproduced in any manner whatsoever without written permission except in the case of brief quotation embodied in critical articles and reviews.

For permission requests, please address:
William Charles Press
7300 W. Joy Road
Dexter, MI 48130

Published by William Charles Press
Printed in the United States of America

ISBN: 978-1-943290-17-8

This publication is designed to provide accurate information as the author recalls her life. The names of most of the people are fictional to safeguard privacy. The author and publisher specifically disclaim responsibility for any liability, loss or risk, personal or otherwise, which is incurred as a consequence, directly or indirectly from the use and application of the contents.

To Ted for his patience and encouragement.

Acknowledgements

Thanks to Reverend Linda Whitworth-Reed, Dr. Charles Monnin Jr., Murli and Mona Mulwani, Janet Harris, Sachse-Wylie Authors Group, Beta readers, cheerleaders, and all who supported me.

A special thanks to Margaine Carity Déléage for the phone number which changed my life forever.

Contents

Prologue 1

Part One — The Gift of the Gray Suitcase

  1: Finding a Friend in London 5

  2: Paris Without Clothes 11

  3: Lyon Letdown 17

  4: Settling into Chambon 23

  5: Acceptance 31

  6: Travel to Le Puy en Velay 37

  7: Explaining the Accident 43

  8: A Bittersweet Birthday 49

  9: Searching for the Suitcase 53

Part Two — Doing the Right Thing

  10: The Suicide 63

  11: The Young Military Couple 65

  12: Facing My Worst Fear 69

  13: Baggage Gone: Dating On 75

  14: Two Stepping to Texas 81

15: Coping...........................87

Part Three—A Passion Travel

16: Tripping in Paris 95

17: The Phantom in Our Family........103

18: Planning the Pilgrimage...........109

19: Morris and Max..................119

20: The Faux-Pas 129

21: The Bridge in Avignon 135

22: The Pilgimage 139

Part Four—Acceptance

23: In Doc's Own Words..............153

24: The Phone Call...................161

25: Gift of the Bucket List.............165

Prologue

"Bill, a letter from Ruth arrived. She made it to Lyon, but she lost her suitcase on the boat while crossing the English Channel. Our precious daughter has only the clothes on her back. She's running around naked in France. What should we do?"

"Now, Florence, she's not naked. I'm sure she can find clothes to wear somehow. She won't want to return because her suitcase is missing. What happened?"

The saga started with my graduation with a major in French from Ohio State University in Columbus, Ohio. I received a heavy, gray American Tourister suitcase and a round-trip ticket to fly to London and take the train to Paris and then to Lyon for my summer job. I didn't care about the suitcase. I cared about the ticket. Risking the solo trip to France started my path to discover losing baggage is not always a loss.

Part One

The Gift of the Gray Suitcase

Chapter 1

Finding a Friend in London

I watched the plane taxi to a stop at the small, dingy Columbus, Ohio airport in 1965. My worried, dare I say distraught, parents hung as close to each other as possible, as I waved a happy, hearty goodbye to board the airplane into my new life.

My parents both worked, while I studied, played several musical instruments, and enjoyed my social life in college. With a major in French and a minor in Psychology and my contract to become a high school French teacher in the fall, the trip began. My parents' gift of a mammoth, gray, American Tourister suitcase contained underwear, a nice dress, casual skirts and slacks, two pairs of shoes, and a white Bible to guide me, (another gift from my parents). I think I added the book *Europe on $5 a Day* and a couple of mysteries in the mix. I had convinced my parents I needed a trip to France to achieve stardom in the classroom.

I winged my way to the Philadelphia airport. I looked forward to staying overnight in the dirty, depressing town of Camden, New Jersey with Nora, my former college roommate, before my flight to England the next day. Nora and I both majored in French and we shared major plans for our lives during the year we lived together at Ohio State University. She wanted an advanced degree in French. I had signed a contract to teach French at a Cincinnati high school when I returned from abroad.

Nora's family came from Italy. As a first generation American, her cultural background and mine differed, but our personalities clicked. When she heard about my ticket to London, she invited me to visit before boarding the plane to my future.

The flight to London left the next morning from the Newark Airport. Her miniscule, Italian mom drove me to the airport, calming my increasing nerves about traveling alone to London, Paris, and onward to Lyon, France, for my summer job. My nausea felt like a huge wad of chewing gum in my stomach. Nora's mom commented on my pallor.

The itinerary took me from the Newark, New Jersey airport to London Heathrow. The itinerary allowed for a hotel with two nights in London. Then I would board a train to Folkestone on the English Channel. I looked forward to the ferry to Calais, France with the next train to Paris. I had reservations at a small hotel in Paris for two days.

The last step took me to Lyon where I would work for the summer *au pair* for a young, American couple. I had worked part time for the wife, filing and answering phones at Ohio State. Her summer job entailed working as an assistant for a French professor whom she met and supported at Ohio State University. She needed a nanny. Her husband would be working on his PhD dissertation.

Overjoyed by the new adventure in my life, I jabbered incessantly on the way to the airport, but the weight in my stomach grew. The suitcase held my possessions, such as the ticket that would take me down my path with many upcoming surprises and challenges.

Sleep arrived in spurts. The airplane creaked noisily, creating a stuffed nose, keeping me awake most of the night. Even in 1965, the seats were none too cushy. By the time I landed at the Heathrow Airport, my hands looked like something from a horror movie. I pulled my hangnails from nervous energy, leaving my fingers bloody ugly.

Somehow I managed to find the train to Paddington Station in London. Fatigued from the flight but stimulated by the rush of people in the architectural wonder of the train station, I collected my bags and began the trek to the hotel. I walked for miles on the misty, sunless day. The old, gray or beige buildings seemed to lean towards me, a little overpowering. I stood on the corner looking at my maps until I discovered I should take a bus.

By the time I reached the cheap, small, colorless hotel, I realized the large suitcase caused back strain. The hotel served its purpose for the night with a clean and comfortable bed.

In the stairwell of the hotel, I met Lucy, who also traveled alone. Lucy reminded me of a dragon-fly with her long, wispy hair and flowing, floppy skirt. We spent the next day, dashing across the city to see London Bridge and other sites, in the misty, blue fog along the pristine Thames River.

My new friend hailed from Massachusetts and was going to visit an aunt in Northern France. She had finished two years of teaching elementary art, where she traveled between several elementary schools weekly. We had much in common and nothing in common but both of us appreciated our new companionship, agreeing we would meet again during our French adventures. Her northeastern accent, perky attitude, and audacious personality helped me maintain shaky stability, rather than being overwhelmed or frightened.

It mostly rained with an occasional burst of sunshine in the afternoon. Lucy and I visited the Tower of London, Westminster Abby, and the Changing of the Guard. Big Ben kept watch over us as we ate along the Thames River. I kept pinching myself in disbelief. We walked from Trafalgar Square to see Westminster Abby in its Gothic splendor. When we entered the Abby, my thoughts turned to my parents, both musicians. Lucy and I could hear someone at the organ, practicing—quite a thrill to my ears. We trailed behind a tour, listening to the local guide explaining the history. The stained glass windows towered above us with bits of sunlight poking through the glass on the bevy of tourists below.

Awed by the centuries-old glory before our eyes, but quite hungry, Lucy and I devoured bland English food at lunch and drank tea with milk later that afternoon. Iced tea might have hit the spot as the sun warmed the day. I wished I could stay, but France called sweetly to keep moving forward. Laughter and smiles reigned while we lingered over soggy fish and chips in a nearby pub as quiet fog descended on the city.

Lucy and I hugged tightly the next day with a promise

to stay in touch, a difficult task with the expense of telephone service in the mid-1960s. She took a different ferry across the Channel.

I enjoyed watching the choppy waves to Calais with the smell of salty water wafting in the breeze. Birds flying behind the ferry shrieked at the travelers for fish, thinking we were fishermen. My stomach rolled with the waves, but my spirit soared with the birds, fantasizing the sites in Paris and Lyon. I breezed through Calais on the train to Paris after debarking the ferry.

Chapter 2

Paris Without Clothes

I was not yet twenty-two with confidence and apprehension about the trip. I had memorized the route to Lyon, but the heavy, gray suitcase caused a little consternation. The suitcase and I would travel from Folkestone on the west side of the Channel to Calais, making our way to Paris, so I thought. What I needed was a backpack, yet I carried only a small purse with my passport, a small map of Paris, and money to exchange. A larger, boring, beige bag with woven handles held underwear, a T-shirt, a lipstick and my contact lens case. My mother insisted I take "a change of clothes, just in case you lose your suitcase."

When I arrived in Paris, the suitcase had disappeared en route from London. Gone. Nowhere to be found. I was alone with the clothes on my back and a T-shirt, as the weather turned as gray as cement. Because I was an only child with overly protective parents, calling home for advice flashed through my mind. But I quickly discarded the thought. I'd cope. Failure was not an option.

Somehow I managed to maneuver through the subway,

after purchasing an ID card and reading the French directions without sobbing loudly. I arrived safely at the little, dingy hotel, where I had made a reservation in advance. The small map of Paris aided my fearless path to the hotel near *L'Opera*. The elevator to the second level surprised me, being so tiny compared to American elevators. *Maybe losing the suitcase was fortuitous*, I thought, as I returned to the problem of no clothes.

After a tasty breakfast with a croissant, strong strawberry jelly and harsh *café au lait* (1/2 hot milk and strong coffee), I wandered through the streets to the Galleries Lafayette to purchase items for survival, clothing to wear. On the way, I exchanged dollars for francs, tucking the newly exchanged francs into my purse. Clothes were outrageously expensive. Understanding the people in the bank occurred without problems. Automated Teller Machines did not exist. I continued the search for clothes.

I don't recall the name of the store where I bought a washable, black knit dress, but it was cheap. The store resembled an American S.S. Kresges, the pre-cursor to K-Mart. I purchased a lightweight, very inexpensive, navy blue plaid cloth suitcase. I began to wonder why I chose the printed burlap dress for wearing on the airplane. I couldn't wash it, because it was too heavy to dry before I left for Lyon. Other items I added to the new, small suitcase included a small bottle of shampoo, toothpaste, a tooth brush, and deodorant, although I recall not many French people wore deodorant.

I checked at the Paris train station later that day to see if my giant suitcase had arrived. That's where I grasped the meaning of the clucking noise of contempt that the French enjoy so much. With a little upturn of his big nose, the short, mustachioed baggage claim employee dismissed me. I wanted to pull his mustache off. I felt sure he could see the worried look on my face. Speaking French at full speed with a shrug of his shoulders, hands in the air, he taught me the term *Chez pas, moi* or "I have no idea." I heard the same phrase over and over during my first adventure to France. That was the day I learned how to put my own nose in the air to explain my lack of knowledge, a trait I carried with me for the rest of my life, especially when I needed to speak French.

I thought about my parents and home. They would be eating lunch when I prepared for bed. I knew they would worry about me. At dusk my fears overpowered me. I had planned to wear the turquois, sleeveless blouse which matched the turquoise and black skirt on my way to Lyon. Instead, I wore my dirty, burlap dress. Positive self-talk helped me with rapid recovery from home sickness. *I can do this. I am doing this. Don't cry. I am an adult.*

While I wandered around Paris, I stopped for a bite of lunch and a handsome, young man approached me with a friendly *bonjour*. He spoke English, French and Arabic, and told me he arrived in France from Morocco. Handsome, swarthy, about my age, he flattered me about my ability to speak French and good looks, which buoyed my spirits. We enjoyed the sunny afternoon wandering the streets of Paris to see the architecture, the Seine River, the cheese shops, and incredible pastries in the windows. The afternoon passed quickly. I was in Paris, hearing the noises of the traffic as it raced through the streets. I recall standing in

Notre Dame, craning my neck to admire the stained glass windows. I loved the largess of the church, the peaceful and quiet atmosphere, coupled with my "personal" tour guide beside me. We walked along the Seine River with its bookstalls and items for tourists. I purchased four prints: *Place de la Tertre, Sacré Coeur* Cathedral, *l'Arc de Triomphe,* and *Notre Dame* Cathedral to frame upon my return to Ohio.

My new male friend accompanied me to my hotel to assure I arrived safely. Seeing places from my text books and movies made me smile as I fell into an exhausted sleep, tired and eager for more sightseeing before leaving on the next leg of the journey.

I awoke to sunshine and my dirty dress, eager to see the Louvre, the Montmartre area, and the inside of *Sacré Coeur* before I departed for Lyon. Shock awaited me at the door. The Moroccan "prince" stood by the front door, wanting to accompany me, which scared me to death. I'd read about "white slavery." I told him to go away. I shook my finger at him, telling him I wanted to be alone for my sightseeing. He followed me. Obviously, I had made a terrible mistake in befriending him. Finally I ditched him in the Louvre, by racing wildly through the halls to an exit while he looked for *le petit coin* (rest room).

I relaxed late that afternoon after all the exploration my feet could handle. I walked and walked and walked, ending the afternoon in *Les Jardins de Tuileries*, a huge green park. I tasted my first *citron pressé* or lemonade. I felt safe seated on a bench with the sun glinting through the trees.

I determined which train would take me to Lyon. Those two days in Paris quelled my fears temporarily, as I knew my summer job awaited me in Lyon. I handled the adversity and had a great adventure.

The next morning, I boarded a train which took about five hours to Lyon. I sat by the windows and watched the sunflowers waving in the light breeze on either side of the tracks. The chance of a lifetime waited for me in Lyon, so I thought. I dozed off and on, relaxed about the loss of my suitcase, excited to start my new job.

I watched some old people on the train unpack their lunches, the aroma of salami and mustard wafting through the air. Babies cried. Children pestered their parents who carried large bags, which I assumed were full of toys and clothes for their destinations. A little girl, about age four, offered me part of her sandwich. The swaying of the train and the sights and the sounds of another country quelled any worries about traveling in a foreign country by myself without my suitcase.

Chapter 3

Lyon Letdown

Norm, the husband, of my former employer at my part-time job, greeted me warmly, holding baby Lisa in his arms. His tiny foreign car dwarfed the Ford Econoline van my dad drove in the U.S. in my small home town of Newark, Ohio. He taught me to drive in his van, a stick shift, which proved to be an asset in France.

Norm's wife, Debbie, had started her job in Lyon two weeks earlier. Her boss lived in Lyon and had spent the last academic year at Ohio State where he taught in an exchange program. He asked her to come to Lyon to support him in a "French as a second language" institute at the University of Lyon. Many Americans would attend the program. Debbie had a basic knowledge of French and had a wonderful reputation with the professor and students in Columbus. She jumped at the chance, but only if Norm and their baby accompanied her. When the professor offered a furnished place to stay for free for the summer, she accepted. Their two bedroom apartment more than served the purpose for the summer. High ceilings, thick brocade curtains, heavy furniture, and a large antique table in the dining room surprised all of us. Debbie told me the apartment belonged to another professor who was traveling for the summer. I dropped my parcels on the floor in the second bedroom which I would share with baby Lisa. I loved the architecture, iron bed and the comfortable reading chair next to Lisa's tiny playpen where she slept.

Norm labored over his dissertation. I don't remember the dissertation topic, but the plan required that I play with and care for Lisa. If I helped with the meals, fine. I would be free to explore Lyon when Lisa slept, while Norm worked in the dining room.

Notes from my diary:

Day 1—Lisa is fussy.
Norm held Lisa most of the day. She slept in spurts. I washed my burlap dress and hung it by the window to dry. The day was sultry and humid, so I'm not sure how long it will take.

Day 2—Lisa is ill.
Norm took Lisa to *le médicin* (doctor) and *la pharmacie* for baby aspirins. Debbie worked late and returned home exhausted.

Day 3—Beautiful day.
Norm worked on his statistics, swearing and grumpy. I

took the baby in *la poussette* (stroller) to the park. I felt lonely among the many moms, few dads and nannies. My slinky, black dress looked quite odd, but I stuck my nose in the air and pretended I was French.

Day 4—Norm complains.

Norm and Debbie didn't need a nanny. The baby slept much of the day. Norm wanted to talk rather than work on his research paper. *Oh, dear,* I thought, *This job is not going to work. I want to escape before intimacy may rear its ugly, snaky head. When he told me he loves my curly red hair I didn't like it one bit. What was he thinking?*

Before I left for my European adventure, I visited my favorite, most influential high school teacher in my home town of Newark. Miss Rodgers, my French teacher, held great prestige in my eyes, as she was my role model, my confidant, my friend. She introduced me to Marie, a high school exchange student, who lived with a family on the same street as mine. Marie, a sweet, gentle French girl of 16, came from le Chambon-sur-Lignon in Central France.

Marie empathized with my jitters about traveling alone to Lyon. She experienced fear and tense muscles when she left her village in the province of Haute Loire, France. Her mother, like mine, worried about her. Marie gave me her mom's telephone number and said, "If you run into any difficulties, call my mother. She will help you."

I don't think Marie and I talked more than an hour, yet the meeting became fiercely important in my life. I couldn't believe she would reach out to someone she didn't know well without checking with her mother. She trusted me enough to share her home number with me. I still remember her sparkling, chocolate brown eyes and smooth mahogany-colored hair. She was mature for her age, understanding and encouraging.

On day five Debbie came home early. The strained atmosphere between Debbie and Norm created more doubt about remaining with the job. I pondered calling the exchange student's mom.

I struggled mightily, trying to decide what I should do. I would not, could not, and should not go home! *Non!* No! *Jamais!* Never! I called Marie's mom in Chambon.

Mme Carity seemed pleased to help me. *Venez ici. Prenez les deux trains, l' un a Lyon, l'autre a St. Étienne à Chambon.* (Come here. Take two trains, one from Lyon and the other from St. Étienne to Chambon). She accepted me without thought. Marie might have told her about our visit, but I'm sure her mother never expected to hear from me. Yet she welcomed me, as if I were her daughter. I told her I'd call her after I talked with Debbie and Norm.

Our conversation was friendly, but awkward. "Debbie, Ruth's right," Norm mumbled. A big man, a little bloated, even at age twenty-eight, he had a resonate voice that now sounded like the bleat of a lost sheep. I told them since Lisa required little care at four months old, they could save money without me. Norm could work and take care of Lisa with his flexible schedule. I did not voice my fear, but I still thought Norm would eventually want my friendliness to go towards their lovely bedroom. When the baby slept, he often "took a break" from his dissertation. He never hit on me, but any twenty-eight-year-old man with a tired wife could be tempted, from my perspective. Why he'd be interested in a boney redhead with freckles and frizzy hair is beyond me, but I was wise enough to see shadows lurking in the corners.

Debbie seemed elated that Norm would care for Lisa, but her face showed remorse, as none of us expected the situation to evolve in disaster for me. All of us felt sad about the situation, but with Chambon available, the relationships would be salvaged. Debbie and I cried and hugged each other the night before I boarded the next train on my life's journey. In the morning, she left for work before I said goodbye to Lisa and Norm.

When I called Mme Carity to tell her when I'd arrive, she agreed to meet me at Le Chambon-sur-Lignon train station. She talked faster in this conversation. She mentioned a possible place where I might work and stay for the rest of the summer. Before I left, my dress had dried, and I had purchased a shirt and more underwear. I worried whether Chambon would have retail stores.

I am grateful to Debbie for the invitation to go to Lyon. Her kindness and their patience in allowing me to leave gracefully avoided possible misfortune in the path.

The train ride from Lyon to St. Étienne offered another opportunity to see the beautiful, French countryside with flowers by the tracks and small towns in the distance with hills and mountains hovering under the cloudless sky. A short wait ensued in the small, industrial town of St. Étienne.

I don't know what I expected the train to Chambon to look like, but the tiny train cars reminded me of an image of a toy a child might enjoy, but big enough for people. The windows, pushed up for summer, delivered a healthy breeze as we chugged along the track, swaying back and forth. My stomach churned with excitement and apprehension.

Possibly the train I rode to Chambon

Chapter 4

Settling into Chambon

Marie's mother greeted me warmly, with a hug and a kiss on each cheek, as if we had known each other for years. Marie looked like her mother with her eyes like big brown puddles of kindness. She explained I would be given free room and board where I would stay in exchange for working as an "aide." We drove to a large gray stucco building called *"Les Genêts,"* a home for convalescents and senior citizens.

My thoughts swam furiously upstream with questions. *What does an "aide" do? Who will be my boss? How will I know what to do and where will I stay at night?* Mme Carity and I exchanged pleasantries. "How did you like the little train? Did you enjoy Lyon?"

Her sweet French accent created a sense of strength and awareness of my angst. She spoke slowly for my understanding. She told me nothing of the history of Chambon and shared little about the town or workplace. My head kept spinning. *How will I work without clothes? Will my parents be able to wire money to me? Is this a step in the right direction?*

Les Genêts, postcard from 1965

I am sorry I didn't get to know this gracious woman. As we drove to the nursing home she explained I would be a kind of "helper" at the *"Maison de Retraite et Repos,"* (a home for rest and relaxation) for French citizens and the elderly. It was referred to simply as *"Les Genêts"* In my head, I translated it as a home for tired people, which was not too far from reality. Marie's mom alerted the director before my arrival about my lack of appropriate clothing for work and play.

La Directrice, whose name was Nancy, welcomed me with open arms at the front door of the huge, gray stucco home. "I'm happy you will help us this summer. Half our people are elderly, and half are here for rest and relaxation."

Thus, I began speaking French constantly. We marched on a short tour of the building, through shadowy halls with the aroma of onions and garlic permeating the entire building. The tour ended at the large bedroom, far from the front door. The room, sparse in furniture, but clean, was painted a light gray. Nancy had left a small pile of clothing for me on the bed. I admit the meager garments caused a bit of alarm, as nothing fit and certainly could not be considered "chic." Shoes? My only pair of shoes would suffice for the entire summer.

Although somewhat dazed, I learned the expectations quickly. Responsibilities covered an abundance of learning opportunities. I drove the little, gray, stick shift Citroen to the downtown market most weekdays to collect vegetables, fruit, potatoes, rice and milk for the approximately fifty people in my new home and job. The list of responsibilities varied from day to day. The language immersion led quickly to speaking French with a heavy American accent.

Each morning started by opening the shutters in residents' rooms, to find the summer sunlight waiting to bring smiles to the residents. The home could have been a dreadful place. Instead, the rooms reverberated with joy. The air was fresh, amassed with golden sunbeams. I wandered the property filled with flowers and ground cover. Benches adorned the hilly grounds, providing a chance to sit quietly, to feel free and peaceful.

I wasn't crazy about cleaning the salad or peeling potatoes, but I never, ever complained. I loved going to the market for the chaos and color of the day. Rushing to make the deadlines for putting food on the table allowed rapid improvement in speaking French. When residents mentioned my French accent was improving, my face radiated with enthusiasm. The feeling of community enveloped me like honey and butter on toast.

Les Genêts, as they referred to the building, contained two distinctly different types of people. The elderly lived on one side while the residents on the other side seemed quite healthy and happy. I didn't ask questions, respecting their needs for privacy. I know some recuperated from surgical procedures, needing a peaceful setting for healing. No one acted as if mental health was an issue, but perhaps I was simply unaware. Everyone was ambulatory. I imagined the elderly had no place else to go.

The ladies called me *Mademoiselle Michelle,* as "Ruth" sounds horrid in French, a guttural sound. I hated the sound of it. Since my last name at the time was McMichael, I suggested Michael or the feminine version, *Mlle Michelle.*

I had trouble understanding *Les Pensionnaires,* or the elderly, as many of them spoke a type of countrified or regional French, termed "Patois." The old folks liked having a young person in their midst. I became attached to a few in a very short time. I remember one skinny, old man, who dressed in an old, red shirt most of the time, sitting with a cane in the foyer; he would smile and mumble something when I would pass. I never understood what he said, but he seemed pleased with my returned smile and cheery *merci*.

The people on the rehabilitation side became my friends. Looking back, I wish I had asked more questions.

La Directrice, about age forty, provided excellent leadership with a direct approach to duties. She was a no-nonsense type with short dark, salt and pepper hair, thin build, and a fast walk. She delegated with authority and wisdom to her tiny staff of two, along with managing the employees who worked part time with the cleaning and food preparation. Getting to know her developed slowly.

The first day, when she led me to my room, she reiterated that I would not be paid, but could stay until I returned to the U.S. in late August. I would receive free room and board for my assistance. Christine, another young woman, shared the same duties as I did, helping with whatever needed to be accomplished. Christine mentioned she was Jewish and attended a university in northern France. We became instant friends.

Conversations delivered a cacophony of noise for me in the dining room. I could not differentiate the various conversations the first week. I was lonely, but happy, to have a wonderful place to stay. Gradually, the words and phrases began to make sense. Table conversation became pleasant, with news of upcoming visits from relatives and friends. Brigitte's daughter might be coming the following weekend or Girard's son would be stopping for coffee. I dreamed in French by the time I left for the United States.

Christine, the other staff member, had long black hair worn in thick braids or pigtails. She majored in Philosophy, was very mature for her nineteen years, and was known to laugh loudly and work diligently. Working at *Les Genêts* was her summer job. I never asked her how she arrived in Chambon. Her good-natured personality added humor and depth to conversations.

We took care of Whiskey, the resident dog, the most spoiled animal in the world. He was a big, scruffy, smelly mutt with hair as wild as mine, only not quite as curly. His muddy beige fur did not shed. He owned the place and the residents adored him. His bed was the couch in the hall, rather than a pillow or a dog house. Christine and I covered his couch nightly with an old, rather dirty, patchwork quilt, putting him "to bed" for the night after dinner. He preferred scraps and leftovers from the delicious meals cooked in the monstrous kitchen filled with the smells of garlic, beef, and other vegetables for soup, simmering on the stove. Whiskey did not smell nearly as good as the aromas in the kitchen.

Whatever we had for lunch went into a giant mixer to make soup for the evening meal. I especially liked the mushroom soup, full of sweet onions and garlic. And of course, bottles of red table wine adorned the tables. No one drank too much. After bedding the dog, we would all be dragging, but would find time for conversation.

One hot summer afternoon, not long after I arrived at *Les Genêts*, Christine and I, working together in the large, empty kitchen, began talking about the beauty of the little town.

"Christine, I'm curious. What makes Chambon exceptional?" I asked in my fractured French.

"Do you mean the mountains, the plateau or the flowers?"

"No, the people. The townspeople who work here and the residents who seem so accepting and friendly."

"I'm not sure. Do you know the history of this town? Maybe that's it."

"I don't know anything about the history. But I'm curious. I noticed the church by the bridge with the letters carved over the door which say "Love one another."

"I know fragments of the history; the people don't talk about it often. During the war this town saved 3,000 or more Jewish children, adults, and people who resisted the war."

"You must mean during World War II, not the Viet Nam War in Asia right now?"

"Absolutely. The townspeople hid the children in their homes and barns, any place safe to keep them from the gas chambers. Some attended *Le Collège Cévenol*, founded by a minister right before the war started. I guess he predicted the future by creating a safe place for the Jewish children."

"We'd better move faster. It's time to warm the soup and start putting the dishes on the table." The aroma of the stew began to fill the room.

"We'll talk more."

That evening Christine traveled the halls, shouting to all to come to the large meeting room after dinner. We had no time to discuss history, as she taught us how to dance the "Hora," which is an old Jewish song and dance, still played at many Jewish weddings around the world. I can still hear the words clearly with the tune still ringing in my head. . . *hava, nagila hava*, (Let's rejoice, let's rejoice, and be merry). Step, put your left foot back of your right, step, now left foot over your right, step and reverse. I don't recall the *"pensionnaires"* dancing, but the other residents laughed and danced until after dark.

I went to sleep thinking about what Christine told me. How did the children find Chambon? Gas chambers? I had studied the history of the war, of course, but it always seemed remote, with little effect on my life. My dad served in World War II when I was a baby, but the gas chambers?

I knew a little, not a lot. Should I ask more questions? Was this common throughout France during the war, to hide Jewish children? I needed more information, but I decided not to look like *The Ugly American*, a popular book about that time. I thought I might look stupid or overbearing or too inquisitive.

Chapter 5

Acceptance

Nancy, *La Directrice*, asked me if I'd like to audit a class at the nearby *Collège Cévenol* as the school had many foreign students, especially in the summer. "Would you like to take a class in the afternoons?" She indicated Marie's mom had called to suggest the plan. I was busy in the mornings fetching the food and helping with preparations for the meals, but in the afternoons I wandered about the small town aimlessly. Soon I would be sitting in the middle of a nearby field on an old blanket practicing French idioms.

As I settled into Chambon, a sense of wonder awoke in me. I was accepted. I was learning and growing. The climate, the culture, and the companionship overwhelmed me with the willingness of all to adopt someone different from them.

Completing the forms for Collège Cévenol took five minutes. The nearby College, about a mile away, required a quick walk across fields. I would not have much time for studying French, but when the opportunity arose, I accepted. The gloomy old gray international school buildings looked their age, dreary but impressively "collegiate." I

Building at Le Collège Cévenol

did not mingle with the young summer-school students, but sat in the rear of the classroom, taking notes while trying to be invisible. What if the professor called on me?

Nancy explained that a local minister established the school during the war when the townspeople hid children from the Nazis. Those children, whom the Nazis wanted to send to internment camps, attended this institution with Jewish and non-Jewish instructors. I continued to neglect asking questions to delve deeper into its history. Marie's mother would have been about sixty when I lived in Chambon. I learned later she and her husband played significant roles in saving many children, but sadly I didn't know the questions to ask my new friends.

I recall hearing about the minister, André Trocmé, an inexhaustible man of righteousness, and his wife. They organized most of the town in an effort to shield the Jewish children whose parents sent them for safe haven during the war. Frequently, Magda Trocmé met the train and found homes for the youngest or boarding houses for the school-aged students. Many arrived in the middle of the night. Some walked into Chambon. Many local families harbored several children.

In the afternoons when I had no class, I took a blanket into the fields of flowers on the path to the College. I don't recall what flowers grew in the fields I crossed. Not grapevines, but maybe yellow *genêts* which are a yellow scrub brush for making brooms. One golden afternoon, I sat on a borrowed blanket, smelling the fresh mountain air, the warm sun upon my shoulders, reading my *French as a Second Language* textbook. My yellow and gray checkered skirt, about four sizes too big, secured with a huge, safety pin, ballooned around me.

A tiny spec of dirt interfered with my contact lens. As I mopped tears with the edge of my skirt, a contact lens popped out. I panicked. Absolutely panicked! I realized that impaired sight might mean an early return trip to Ohio. I looked on the blanket. I looked under the nearby flowers, not standing up to avoid stepping on the lens.

Something glinted in the sun on a black rock by my side. My lens! I spit on my contact lens, put it in my eye, and returned to work. Life is full of big and small surprises.

Within the next few days, I suffered painful awareness of my lack of knowledge. The Viet Nam War raged. Controversy and peace marches happened on most campuses, including Ohio State.

The younger residents would often sit outside under a blanket of stars, talking and laughing after dinner. Sometimes, Christine joined us. Most of the time, I chimed in to the conversations. One evening, one of the ladies questioned me about Viet Nam. I paid little attention to the Viet Nam War, after leaving the university, but I knew I was against war.

"Michelle, why is the U.S. supporting South Viet Nam in the war?" Danielle asked. I didn't have a clue, but tried to muddle through an answer.

Another resident commented, "Michelle, I have pictures of the buildings where the U.S. dropped bombs on my city during World War II. I don't hold it against you or the soldiers, but my uncle died in one of the air raids." We talked about Viet Nam and World War II as my French friends' curiosity bubbled with the opportunity to discover what Mlle Michelle thought.

"Michelle, do you understand they saved maybe 5,000 children and adults from the gas chambers in Germany in this little town?"

Gretchen, who migrated from Germany, spoke French with a slight German accent. She shared that her oldest brother lived in Chambon during the war and attended Cévenol. She said she thought he arrived on the same train as I, clutching only a small bag with a half-eaten sandwich and a note with directions to find Chambon. Marie's mother might have directed him to the farm where he helped with the crops to feed all who arrived at the little train station.

"My brother and two other children hid in the fields behind the barn when the police or soldiers arrived nearby." Gretchen shared his story.

Chambon was situated on the north edge of the Resistance to German occupation. The German soldiers stayed in a nearby town. Often, the soldiers seemed to look the other way. They knew about the Trocmés' efforts for the Resistance.

"Gretchen, are you Jewish? Isn't this town Huguenot? Why did they take care of the children?" I asked.

"The Huguenots lived their pacifism. My brother said a man named Andre Trocmé, their minister, began preparing the town starting in the late 1930s, telling the residents the children would come. He hired Jewish instructors to teach at *Le Collège*, which might have saved their lives."

"Why did parents send their kids to Chambon?"

"Only by word of mouth. Cousins told cousins. Uncles told Grandmas. Danger lurked in all of France."

Little by little, I learned, but failed to recognize the significance of the history. I thought all the little towns hid children and adults if they abhorred the concentration camps and deadly gas chambers. Later, I discovered people might harbor three or four children in towns throughout France, but Chambon seems to hold the record for thousands of people saved from the Gestapo and worse.

"Why would the townspeople put themselves in jeopardy?" I asked. "Didn't they fear they would be exterminated, too?"

"No, they believed in a simple truth of righteousness and kindness. They don't talk much about it, but they did the right thing."

Huguenot history demonstrates love and peace. They experienced persecution for centuries in Europe. The strong leadership of the Trocmés and his team of mighty men and women of Chambon supplied the strength and willpower to "do the right thing." One person specialized in forging identification papers and changing last names to hide their ethnicity. The Goldstein name became *D'Or* or Rubenstein to *Raimbaud*. Finding shoes and clothes for the children, as their feet and bodies grew, the townspeople tackled, especially during the winter months. Food became scare. Farmers in the area supplied food when possible to assure the children survived. The entire town knew how to stretch food by "putting another potato in the pot," a favorite saying, when the children arrived on their doorsteps. The history is fascinating and heroic, but I failed to realize that during my first visit.

My answers to their questions lacked depth. I didn't grasp much about wars or history. My mission to learn the language and cultural norms centered my life. I understood little of the massive loss of life in Viet Nam or World War II. I had protested the Viet Nam War on the Ohio State Campus. Television showed me that war is deplorable, yet history keeps repeating. My new friends lived in cities where bombing occurred during World War II. They lived the experience, while I simply viewed the tragedy of Viet Nam on television.

Their questions helped me to mature that summer. I didn't realize the power my trip to Chambon would yield in my future. War? Why war? Why can't people accept each other?

The people of Chambon opened their doors to all who came. When I arrived, they opened their doors to me. They fed and clothed me. They offered a place to stay and work. Their kindness and support left me wondering what I would do under the same circumstances.

Chapter 6

Le Puy en Velay

Nancy, *La Directrice*, departed *en vacannes* (on vacation) three weeks later, announcing that her temporary replacement would be Monique. Although Christine, my co-worker, and I liked Nancy, Monique's demeanor sparkled by comparison. Her friendliness immediately won our hearts and gave us a desire to please. Sometimes I struggled to understand her sense of humor as jokes could be a "play on words," which I simply didn't understand. But I laughed heartily, despite my obliviousness.

Monique, divorced with no children, held no secrets or reservations. She was tall, thin, with short reddish-blond hair and dazzling blue eyes. We enjoyed her stay for about five weeks. She arrived from Paris where she worked as a nanny, eager to try the temporary assignment. We rarely talked about her life, but Christine and I agreed that Monique was a breath of fresh air. Her energy improved the tedious tasks for Christine and me, tasks such as peeling potatoes. She sang little French songs in the kitchen as we worked. As we sang *"Sur la Pont d'Avignon,"* I yearned to visit Avignon, farther south in France.

When Monique heard the story of my unexpected arrival in Chambon on the little train, she decided to take Christine and me to Le Puy, less than a half-day drive from Chambon. The three of us set out to see the nearby countryside in the *deux chevaux* or "two horses," the resident Citroen.

We squished into the Citroen with Monique driving. Fortunately, no accidents occurred regardless of the twists and turns on the mountainous terrain, with Monique speeding as a race car driver in the Grand Prix. The mountains, although not terribly steep, rose like giant, tan spikes from the volcanic age. The green trees and foliage arising out of the rocks created unique scenery. Round and round the bends we flew, flashing through the colorful countryside. It was a day trip and a happy event to remember forever. Volcanoes formed the region long ago with strangely shaped pinnacles and a myriad of brown rock formations.

Catholic churches abound around Le Puy, but the astounding shadow of *St. Michel d'Aiguilhe*, the rock formation, termed a "needle," gave us pause to view its majesty. The peasants began building the monument in the year 962 as a sacred place for pilgrimages. I was awestruck with the history of the region since the United States didn't exist at that time. My home town seemed remote that day. Ohio State University faded from my reality.

At the base of St. Michel's needle, old ladies in traditional garb made lace. Monique explained, "Lace is an industry in this area. Pilgrims wind their way to this small town from all over the world." People climb to the top with 286 steps to achieve blessings for their efforts. With our time limitations on our escape from Chambon, we decided not to climb

Postcard from the trip to Le Puy-St. Michel
in lower right

to the top, where a Chapel sits, built in the twelfth century. Religious pilgrims and other visitors buy lace in the stores and from these ladies: tablecloths, bedspreads, stuffed animals, all hand-made.

Although I lacked much money, I bought a souvenir: a small doll from one of the old women who had dressed her in red satin, edged with the lace of the area. It remains a treasure on my bookshelf.

We wondered how the workers built the church on top of the rock. The view from the top must be spectacular, overlooking the small town. What a treat, both the souvenir and the memories.

We ate ham and cheese sandwiches on hard rolls at a picnic table along the side of the road. The breeze, in the heat of the hot July day, kept us cool. Monique insisted she teach us more French children's songs. On the way back to Chambon, I learned "She'll be Coming Round the Mountain" in French. The translation wasn't exactly what I learned as a child. The next to last stanza translated, "She was kissing her grandfather on the way down." The last stanza sent us into gales of laughter as the translation is. "I'd like to be her grandfather on the way down the mountain." I can still sing every word of that French song.

Although Monique's driving scared me, she told Christine and me a little about her childhood, growing up in Paris during World War II. Her bubbly personality diminished into sobering tones as we ate our lunch.

"Do you know about *Vel d'Hiv* or the *Vélodrome d'Hiver*? Do you know about what happened to the Jews in Paris twenty-three years ago? I'm not sure many Americans know how horrific the war was. I was a little girl. In July of 1942, the French police, with orders from Hitler's leadership, gathered over 10,000 Jewish people to send to the gas chambers. Women, children, and teenagers were forced into this big stadium. No food, little water, no bathrooms. It was terrible."

"Are you Jewish?" I asked.

"My dad was Jewish. He went to Auschwitz and never came back. We felt fortunate to survive. My mom and brothers escaped when a French police officer looked the other way, but let's not talk about this. The memories bring tears to my eyes. I was ten, but understood that both the police and Gestapo would kill all of us if we failed to follow their orders." We drove in silence until we reached Chambon.

Later, I read more about *"Vel d'Hiv,"* which indicated 38,000 Jews were killed at Auschwitz, including 3,000 children.

I have no idea how the residents managed without us that day, but as far as we could tell they coped. Our adventure brought us closer as a team. We needed the break in routine.

As we reached the town, I realized Chambon provided far more education for me than Lyon with new friends and sightseeing like a native. Without my decision to resign my nanny job, my adventure in Chambon would never have happened. I read American history books and studied French history, but failed to realize the magnitude of World War II. Without petite Monique, I might not have learned about *Vel d'Hiv*. Christine and I greatly missed Monique when she returned to Paris.

Chapter 7

Explaining the Accident

"Christine, Christine!" I yelled. "I received a letter from Lucy, my friend from Massachusetts. I mean, the friend I met in London who is from Massachusetts. We traveled together to Paris. She wants to visit Chambon and take trains to Switzerland for a weekend. Would Nancy allow me to leave for the trip? Do you suppose Lucy could stay with us?"

"Why not ask her? You may never see Switzerland otherwise. Your mama would not want you to go alone. The worst Nancy can say is *non*."

"Would she be upset? I would be gone the entire weekend. And Lucy wants to visit us to see the area. I want to show her Chambon, but I have no money to pay for her to stay here."

Timidly, I approached Nancy who had returned the previous week from her vacation. She seemed far more relaxed than before her vacation.

"Mademoiselle," I began. "I met a new friend in London who traveled with me to Paris. She plans to leave her relatives to return to the United States soon. She sent me a letter to see if she might come to Chambon and stay with me for a few days. My room is big enough for two. Could she stay with us two days? She will travel to Switzerland for a weekend after visiting Chambon."

"D'accord!" (Of course!) When will she be here? Perhaps you would like to travel a little with her. You mentioned your parents sent a little spending money. If she wants you to go to Switzerland with her for a few days, no problem." I had worried needlessly.

Lucy arrived at the Chambon rail station on the little train, toting a small bag for our travel adventure. We served breakfast and toured the town. I showed her the *Le Collège* and mentioned about how the town saved many children during the war. Neither of us thought much about what that meant, but she said she had heard about it in a French class.

As we walked around the village, she shared a bit of French history.

"Ruth, I had a wonderful European history class, but I may not have the dates quite straight. When France succumbed to Germany in the early 1940s, Henri Pétain was appointed to rule Central France, which they called Vichy, the un-occupied area where few Germans reigned in the surrounding area. I think Pétain lived in a nearby town. He had served in World War I as a strong leader and warrior for France. Pétain became a puppet of Hitler's, arresting people, sending them to internment camps and making life miserable. The "Resistance" happened in many parts of Central and Southern France. Your story about the 5,000 Jewish people saved in Chambon makes sense. Later, Pétain was tried for treason and barely escaped death. He finished his life on an island somewhere, in shame. But during the first part of his Vichy reign, his soldiers looked the other way. They must have realized what was happening in Chambon."

Lucy and I decided to go to Geneva, taking the train through the eastern mountains of France to the international landmark, situated on the southwest tip of Lake Geneva. Although I had become much more comfortable understanding French conversations, I tired easily from the effort. My time with Lucy refreshed my resolve to learn more about the area and travel frequently. Our conversations helped both of us piece together how difficult life became during the war.

We took *le petit train* to St. Étienne, another train to Lyon and still another train to Geneva. The trains hustled through the dazzling countryside. The mountains kept "growing" as we traveled. We gazed out the window as the train rocked on its rails through deep ravines in the mountains, then climbed to new heights. The flowers in the fields beside the tracks shook their blue, pink, and purple heads at us, waving in the wind. We ate the lunches we had packed in Chambon, carried in our string bags called *les filets*. The church steeples in each small town stood taller than trees. I wanted to stop in every little town in the valleys. *Someday*, I thought, *I want to return to see more of Switzerland.*

The weather cooperated for our short trip. Lake Geneva shimmered in the sunlight with stunning architecture surrounding us. Lucy departed to visit a former boyfriend who lived on the north side of Geneva. The United Nations' building where human rights conferences meet towered above. Geneva is a noisy, super clean city. I wandered around, listening to a multitude of languages in the streets. I sat alone near a dock on Lake Geneva, eating a sandwich. As I watched the *Jette d'Eau de Genève* (Geneva Water Fountain) in the distance, I said a prayer of thanks for the opportunity to see where hope for peace exists on a daily basis, to see the mecca for peaceful existence.

Lucy arrived later that afternoon, hobbling, after a car, going too fast, hit her as she crossed a busy street. The car failed to stop at a crosswalk. Was she ok? Could she travel by herself when we split in opposite directions? Her right leg turned shades of black and blue with lime, yellow and purple surrounding the knee. Her ex-boyfriend helped patch her bloody wounds when it occurred. He had insisted on giving her some aspirins to help with pain, plus purchased the Swiss equivalent of an ace bandage. Thank goodness nothing broke, despite a slight limp. As we returned to our dank, but clean, hostel for the evening, our lives stayed on track.

The next day, Lucy and I parted in the immense, gray halls of the train station in Lyon. We hugged and gave each other the three-cheek-kisses to show our adaption to French customs. Two more trains carried me to Chambon. She would return to Paris and fly to New York, retrieving her large suitcase at the train station before going to the airport. We vowed to stay in touch, but we never connected again.

When I returned to Chambon, explaining in French how Lucy suffered bruises when hit by a car proved difficult. I finally said in French, "A car walked on my friend." They understood. I still don't know how to explain it.

The weather turned cooler. As I moved through my duties on Monday I felt pangs of homesickness with summer's end only a few weeks away. The nausea in the pit of my stomach became the sadness I felt at the thought of leaving Chambon, not desire for the return to Ohio.

Chapter 8

The Bittersweet Birthday

The time to leave Chambon approached. My short course at *Le Collège* ended mid-August. I had plans to visit Darmstadt, Germany via Amsterdam to see a military family from my hometown.

Thinking about the return trip, although daunting, excited me, but my mind wavered about leaving my friends in Central France. I wanted to go home, but I wanted to stay in Chambon. The clock kept ticking. The mundane tasks became tedious, although the people surrounding me remained vibrant.

One more week to go. I spoke with the people who sold vegetables to say *"Au revoir."* I shook hands with the meat market man and kissed the flower sales lady on both cheeks to say goodbye. She tucked a small rose in the top buttonhole of my baggy sweater. Who would drive the little, gray Citroen which I used to gather food? I loved driving it. The lonely walks through the big gray building and surrounding neighborhood forced me to face the future.

The night before I left, the ladies surprised me with a

Ruth in the Citroen with a resident

small party and a gift to wish me a happy birthday and *bon voyage*. They collected fifteen francs from the residents to give *Mlle Michelle* an unexpected gift. They knew I owned only two items to wear on my long return trip to Ohio.

I left my borrowed clothes on the bed. The loose-fitting garments remained for others who might arrive on the doorstep of *les Genêts*. They were durable, peasant clothing, useful and weather worn. I would be happy to wear more fashionable clothes again. My old suitcase would be at the train station in Paris, Calais, or Folkestone, I surmised, as I reversed my itinerary.

On the way to the train station, I stopped in the tiny jewelry store on the public square in the center of the village, to purchase a gold-plated Huguenot cross to remind me of Chambon. Most women in the town, and many of my co-workers, wore Huguenot crosses.

My research about the cross concurred with what I knew about the Huguenots, which indicated the cross evolved from their ongoing religious persecution from the 1500s. Although I don't wear the cross daily, people often comment about its beauty.

I hesitated to purchase the cross, as it cost ten francs from my limited funds, but I wanted the cross. The cross would forever remind me of the kindness and generosity of my summer in Chambon.

The *Chambonais* sheltered me, the same as they sheltered the Jewish children. They gave me food and clothing when I needed it. They showed their love, despite my naiveté.

Their fear of the Nazis and Vichy government never kept them from protecting the children in danger during World War II. Their humble, quiet demeanor kept most of them safe during the war, despite the risks they took in hiding children. I fathomed the *Chambonais* packing their fear in a suitcase or deep within their souls until their ordeal ended.

As I packed my thoughts near the end of my time in Chambon, I itemized in my head what I'd learned. I could survive with one pair of shoes. I functioned without nice clothing. But I don't think I realized the power that the experience had played within my heart. Love your neighbor. Love all people: country people, disabled, depressed, stupid, religious fanatics; we are to love unequivocally.

Sometimes when I hear conservative or radical Christians trying to "save souls," I recall the *Chambonais*:

they didn't preach about Jesus, but demonstrated Christian love for all.

As I walked to the train station from the nursing home, a light shower erupted, but the rain stopped in less than five minutes. An orange glow peeped through the departing raindrops, and I noticed a magnificent rainbow. I boarded the tiny train for the last time, alone, happy and full of hope for the future. I tucked away fear of the future. The rainbow was shining for me. I fantasized returning to Chambon in the future.

Chapter 9

Searching for the Suitcase

The wheels of the tiny train rolled down from the plateau through the hills and valleys to St. Étienne. Late August brought a tinge of fall to the air with a few trees showing yellow tips on their leaves. I waited briefly for my train. I had no desire to wander on this part of my journey.

I purchased my ticket to Lyon, waited for the train to appear, carrying my navy blue and green plaid suitcase, lightweight with few items. I had celebrated my twenty-second birthday and had increased my confidence with my travels. Yet, deep down, I shuttered with nervous tension about seeing my friends in Germany. And finding my suitcase.

Once I arrived in Lyon, the train to Paris would depart in fifteen minutes, requiring a sprint to the boarding location, after buying another ticket. The train going north for my trip to visit Holland and Germany would not require crossing Paris to another station. Thankfully, the ticket line was short. I decided not to look for my luggage when I passed through Paris to go to Holland and Germany. As I thought about it, the best chance to find it might be in Calais on my way across the Channel to London and onward to Ohio. I surmised my camera still rested in the big, gray suitcase that I had lost on my trip across the Channel.

The sultry day in Paris alleviated any remorse about leaving Chambon. Finding the right boarding *quai* (boarding platform) took more time than I expected, but I found a seat, once I located the right track. Excitement about the new adventure overshadowed my ambivalence.

The scenery outside my train window enveloped my thoughts. The hues passing quickly kept my heavy eyelids from drooping to sleep. The yellow, green, and blue late summer flowers looked like a Monet painting. I imagined people in wooden shoes charged with building the canals in the Netherlands long ago. How could the hard-working Dutch build homes where nothing existed but water? My thoughts spun as rapidly as the wheels that clattered down the tracks. I dosed sporadically on the train between the happy little towns on my path, despite my desire to visit every village.

As I arrived near dusk in Holland, the paddles on the windmills wound their way around and around in the distance. Here was another picture-perfect moment in my life, with no camera to capture the scenery.

Another big train station in Amsterdam. Another stop on my journey where I wanted to remain unflappable. Within minutes of disembarking with my small suitcase, I stood on a street corner in Amsterdam, crying. I couldn't determine the direction to my hotel. So much for my confidence.

A sweet, old lady with a rosy face and grandmotherly

attitude, stopped to help me. In halting English, she asked if I could speak German. No, I could muster a few Spanish words and converse in French, but no German. Although panicky with no ability to speak Flemish, German or other language she might comprehend, we managed fractured sign language. I had an address which she recognized. My new friend walked the four blocks with me to the hotel. I hugged her like I'd hug my mother upon arrival at my destination. As darkness fell on the windmills and me in Amsterdam, the old lady's kind gesture raised my spirits. She pointed to a restaurant, which I assumed meant she thought I needed to eat.

Later the next morning, I boarded the train to Darmstadt. The short visit to Amsterdam left me with the desire to return, but with a friend or spouse.

Ken, my military friend, met me at the train station. Our bland conversation covered the weather and the ages of his children, which numbered four. I babysat for two of the four children when I attended high school. Before I left Ohio, they asked me to visit, because his aunt told him about my trip. Ken was a "lifer" in the Air Force. I knew other members of his family from my childhood. The evening flew as I became acquainted with the new babies and hugged the two older girls. Speaking English warmed my heart. The joyous evening negated my nervousness about the visit. In the morning, the butterflies arose early, uncomfortably flitting around my stomach, colliding repeatedly, but it was time to go. Ken drove me to the station where a hug from the big, burly man comforted me like a blanket.

The topography was vastly different on my return trip to

Cindy, Mike, Sherry, and Pat.

Paris. I recall the rain poured all day. Watching the weather through the window agreed with my muggy mood.

Upon my arrival at the Gard du Nord train station, I asked (in French, of course) to see their baggage storage area. Disgust registered on the ticket master's face.

"Mlle, you are not allowed to go there."

"But I lost my suitcase when I came across on the ferry from Folkestone to Calais. I want to see if you still have my big gray suitcase."

"Mlle, it would not be here. You must look in Calais if they permit it."

"Are you sure? Really sure?" I demanded.

"*Mais, oui! Certainement.*"

I had learned a bad word in French. "*Merde! Merde! Merde!*" I whispered under my breath. I bet you can translate that.

I boarded the train, stepped off in Calais with my ugly, blue plaid suitcase close at hand, to talk to the baggage people. I met a very short, plump, abrupt, unhappy, Frenchman who appeared to have experienced the death of a loved one earlier in the day.

"*Pardon, Monsieur.* I want to look in your luggage room. Please, I lost my suitcase in June, and I want to find it before I return to America. I need *les trucs* (stuff, things) in it."

I never mentioned the wrath I would incur from my mother if I never found the suitcase. He looked overworked and tired, without any empathy for an American in distress. He would not care about my mother's anger.

I think the baggage steward wanted a short reprieve from his tasks. He led me to the baggage chamber, smoking a foul-smelling cigarette.

"See, your suitcase isn't here," he voiced loudly, as I peeked through the door.

"Let me look around."

The room, about the size of a large American living room, filled with lost luggage in every nook and cranny, loomed eerily somber. I wandered around, aware of the baggage steward's foot tapping and nose in the air. I could see aggravation written all over his face.

"Is this where you keep all lost luggage? There isn't any other place?"

Oui, Mlle. C'est tout. That's all of it.

I refused to give up.

"Are the bags from earlier near the back?"

Naturellement. He snorted.

As I walked to the back of the room, I recognized my American Tourister. My parents would be so pleased. My face fell. How would I manage the monstrous suitcase and two smaller bags? I'd figure it out. I wanted to hug the obnoxious, little man, but I refrained. He smelled terrible and snarled at me. My good feelings about the French became an immediate dichotomy. I love the French. I loved him for letting me look for my suitcase, but I didn't appreciate his treatment or smell.

Calais played a role in World War II. The Germans planned extensively for an invasion from the Allied Troops at Calais, but the invasion occurred in Normandy. The hoax helped end World War II.

Today, when I read about Calais in the news I remember the joy I felt when I retrieved the suitcase in that train station. Calais faces formidable challenges from the influx of migrants wanting to reach England and other destinations as they flee war torn areas. A tent city called the "Jungle" exists outside the town. They say 3,000 or more live in hope of new lives, as did the Jewish people during World War II. Several died trying to exit the country through the tunnel. Calais faces new challenges of historic proportions.

I made a hasty retreat to the ferry to jump on it before it departed, lugging all three bags. My trip from Paris to London happened long before the Chunnel became reality and before the ferry no longer made its voyage back and forth at least four times daily. My journey from Paris to London took about nine hours, I think. Today the TGF fast train takes about 2.5 hours. You can still ride the train-ferry-train but only if you don't mind wasting time, as it still takes forever, compared to the fast trains.

As I remember, I emptied the contents of my purse into the small bag I carried with make-up, pens, and other paraphernalia. I packed much of my clothing into the plaid suitcase. I decided to mail the plaid suitcase home. Finding my way to the London post office with the heavy suitcase created no problem, as I used a locker at the train station to store the big one while I located the post office. Although my money had dwindled to almost nothing, I paid the man at the counter, sadly noting that I would not see this plaid suitcase for six weeks or maybe never. Later the same day, I boarded the plane to New York City. As I weaved through customs, I realized that a chapter in my life had ended. My parents awaited me at home. A friend drove me to Ohio where my mother's first question was, "Did you find your suitcase?"

"Yes, Mother, but I learned that I should pack much less. I didn't need all that stuff. Don't you want to hear about Chambon?" They showed little interest. I was home. They were ecstatic and relieved I returned with no major accidents or tragedies. They expressed surprise that their "little girl" handled the trip with aplomb. Dad shook my hand and hugged me. Mother continued to harbor distaste for my accomplishments. She never understood my love of other cultures and languages.

Eagerly, I trotted off to Cincinnati for my first year of teaching, after repacking my suitcase and charming my father into helping me buy my first car. Not quite grown up, but on my way.

Part Two

Doing the Right Thing

Chapter 10

The Suicide

As a feisty, first-year teacher after my trip to France, I faced abrupt surprises to manage: unmotivated students, political issues with the school leadership, plus long, unappreciated hours of work. I enjoyed the classroom teaching, but the emotional toll exhausted me. Mollie, a second-year French student became the catalyst for my desire for career change.

She looked distressed one day in our French II class. I suggested she visit with me after school. Her grade had dropped an entire letter in the past six weeks. What caused her lack of effort? Mollie, a slightly pudgy, sixteen-year-old with sad eyes, disheveled hair and unfashionable clothes, arrived immediately after the bell rang. After a few minutes of questions, sitting in the stark classroom with posters of the Eiffel Tower and Seine River, she wept about her parents' divorce. She felt responsibility for her mother's weariness because her mom worked several jobs and complained constantly. Often, her mother voiced personal problems, while berating her for not helping more with housekeeping and cooking. When Mollie mentioned suicide, I panicked because I had no training to help her other than finding the suicide prevention number. Mollie survived. I wanted and needed more education to handle situations like Mollie's.

I decided to take a government job while searching my soul for the right decision. I could not afford to return to college, but I made a commitment to return for a counseling degree when possible.

That decision led to a career full of gratifying rewards in helping others. After graduate school, I worked in high school programs as a counselor. The economy faltered. I was laid off each year, but I was called back to work in a pregnant adolescent program and a high school dropout program. I became the lone counselor in a large Catholic high school. Although I loved each job, I began to think about self-employment.

I never regretted my career change. When I packed the old suitcase to move to Texas, I left school systems to start my own company to help adults with their careers. I thought working with adults would be similar and the flex-time would help with family responsibilities. I transferred my skills and background from helping youth to adults. I began to write worthwhile articles and curriculum for careers. I loved my new career.

Chapter 11

The Young Military Couple

I loved Mark within a few weeks of meeting him the summer I left teaching. His dimple and quick quips grabbed my attention the first day we met. I liked everything about him: tall, cynical at times, outgoing, and good looking. Spending time together filled our hearts with discovery of our similarities of views on everything from Camus to camping. We enjoyed movies, hated skiing, and enjoyed the outdoors. Was it really love?

The challenges seemed larger than the peaks of the Alps for both of us. We exchanged passionate, in-depth ideas about the justice of war as Viet Nam continued its ugliness. We discussed our views about similarities and differences in religion. I was Presbyterian and he was Catholic. What would we do about religion and our possible children? What would we do about his military obligation? The Vietnam War news played on the nightly news. Was the war wrong?

His draft papers sat on his desk. Would we move to Canada or would he go to Officers Candidate School (OCS)? We opted for the latter.

My soul-searching helped me decide I could promise to raise our children Catholic, but I could not espouse Catholicism personally. I registered for a class for non-Catholics required before marriage in the Catholic Church. When asked to promise to obey the rules for non-Catholics, I signed the form. My mother began raising hell about the religious differences.

"Mom, please don't worry. Mark and I will always be devoted to Christian principles. It doesn't matter where we marry. Since he's decided to go to Officer's Candidate School, he'll serve two years in the service. Then we can start our real life."

We wanted to marry between Mark's Basic Training and OCS, which seemed to strike the Bishop, or whoever wrote a letter to us, as weird. Correspondence from the Catholic Church arrived stating that a specific date to marry was "inappropriate," not something to do on an "off weekend." Was this a ploy to prevent the marriage? My frustration mounted, not only from my mother's despair about our relationship, but the stress from the Catholics. With the television announcers giving viewers the statistics of the killed and wounded in Vietnam each day, we needed support, not this. People demonstrated against the war in Viet Nam. Flags were burned and politics caused major chaos.

The Catholics attempted another upheaval for us. A second letter arrived stating, in essence, "If you marry in the Catholic Church in your hometown, you must marry in the geographic area where your parents reside." My parents were Presbyterian. What difference would the location of the church or where my parents lived make in God's eyes? We both loved God and each other, but we acquiesced, unknowingly setting the date on the anniversary of his parents' marriage.

Finally, the day arrived with perfect, summer sunshine in small town Ohio. My mother dressed in a beautiful geranium pink dress, rather than the black dress she had threatened to wear. She loved preparing for the reception at my parents' big, century-old home. Despite the anguish during the planning, smiles and congratulations rang as loud as the bells during the ceremony.

The happy couple headed for Columbus, Georgia, for Officers Candidate School. We found a tiny white cottage behind a mansion belonging to a gentle, Georgia couple. Mark's training required staying on base at Ft. Benning. His Catholic background began eroding. During "chapel time," he finagled quick visits to see his darling. I welcomed those few minutes together with open arms.

Life in Columbus, Georgia in 1967 brought new insight, especially for a realistic look at educational values. The Columbus map showed the schools as "W" or "C" for some strange reason. The light dawned when I realized W meant "White" and C meant "Colored." My Mid-western schools were integrated. I began to understand segregation remained alive in the South.

No openings existed in Columbus for French teachers. However, across the state line in Alabama, an opening appeared in a black school where officials mandated integration. Although I opposed segregation, I feared taking the job, because I knew I would be leaving the area within six months. The job might be devastating for relationship building with the students. I thought about the challenges of probable "tokenism." An administrative position near my little abode became available. I vacillated for several days before withdrawing my application for the school position to assuage my guilt. Did I do the right thing? I rationalized the students needed a long-term token teacher, rather than someone who took advantage of the situation for the short-term paycheck.

Military wives stick together. I became friends with several OCS wives. We cooked meager meals to share with each other. The nearby drugstore served hotdogs with the best chili sauce in the South. Oyster crackers on top created a tasty, weekly OCS wives' feast. If the first six months of my marriage indicated the future, I would be happy for the rest of my life.

At the end of Officers Candidate School, we could hear the tearful sounds of "Stay in touch" and "Let me know how it goes" whispered in the wind. How many of their husbands would live or die? None of us knew. And how many of the friendships and marriages would endure.

Chapter 12

Facing My Worst Fear

Our first son arrived while "we" were in the military. When Mark left his military job, he returned to a government job, where his career skyrocketed. I returned to graduate school. In required career counseling and career theory courses, I became "hooked" on a future in career counseling. I loved helping people with their careers. I finished my classes for an M.S. in Counseling and Training the same week my second son popped into the world.

A month later, we moved to Springfield, Illinois. Mark's job required we move four times. When we started the relocation to Minneapolis, trouble hit like splats of large raindrops on a tin roof.

I suspected my husband's attraction to another woman, while he trained for his new job in Minneapolis. The boys, aged two and five, and I remained in Springfield to sell the house. One night on the phone, he mentioned, "I hope you meet Dorothy, when you and the boys get here."

"Oh, who is Dorothy?"

"Dorothy reminds me of you. She's tall, slim, a red-head, just like you."

"Is she in your class?"

"We had dinner together tonight nearby and she's married with two kids, too."

"Does she live in Minneapolis?"

A wife knows. She may not know for sure, but her gut screams the reality to the brain. She suspects. The feeling bubbled up my esophagus to my throat, red-hot and acidic, creating the thought that "men-o-pause" or worse had arrived.

Springtime blossomed in Minneapolis. We purchased a yellow Cape Cod home, not too far from his office. As the boys grew, they loved to climb the crabapple tree outside the kitchen window. The pond across the street gave the neighborhood kids a place to find frogs and pretend to fish. The trees blossomed and cool breezes blew. My little garden produced massive amounts of dark green and yellow squash. In the winter the dog fell through the snow and had to be saved from an avalanche. The kids made snow caves; I hated the winter weather.

I found a job, working part time as a counselor for the Minneapolis Public Schools, in a middle school. I loved the job and living together again as a family, but something was off-key. Mark worked late many nights, often missing dinner. The children missed their daddy. I missed the warmth we shared before the relocation.

At Christmas, the company allowed me a brief encounter with "the other redhead." I remember the creepy, sickening feeling at the company party. As Mark said, she looked somewhat like me, although her brassy, red hair looked dyed to me. I disliked her without understanding her serious problems. What happened to my compassion? I must have packed it in the old gray luggage I still owned, which went to Europe a decade ago.

The marriage evaporated like drops on a lily pad. Mark came home later and later. I suffered gargantuan angst and elephantine tears with the reality of my situation. We argued. I told him he must decide between Dorothy and me. He kept lying, saying he no longer would see her. He chose me, the bum.

He tried to sever the relationship, but she became suicidal. He wavered. I cried more big tears. One night in a drunken or depressive stupor, Dorothy appeared at our home. Our children slept while Mark and I argued in the den.

"Do you want her or me? What are you going to do?" She was crying alligator tears in her car, sitting in front of our home. The children continued to sleep during the fracas. I thought maybe a frying pan over his head could bring him to his senses, but did not act on that momentary urge.

"I want my family. I love her and I love you," he wailed.

"Well, you can't have both, but we can't let her drive in her condition. I'll make coffee so she's fit to drive."

What was I thinking? I wasn't. I was simply doing the right thing. I didn't want her to kill herself or someone else in her condition or inebriation.

Mark talked her into coming inside for discussion. For some strange reason, I took cups from my "good" dishes to serve coffee to the whiney, self-centered "other woman" and tortured husband. Dorothy's face, swollen from crying, looked like she belonged in a morgue. I felt sorry for her pain because we loved the same man and one of us would lose. I wanted to save the enemy's life. What was wrong with me? Serve coffee to the enemy?

Somewhere in the back of my mind, I recalled the evening in Chambon when one of the women at the rest home where I had worked questioned me about Americans bombing France. Americans were the enemy at one point in her life. Now the enemy was in my living room. I tried to treat her as I would have wanted to be treated. I loved no one that night, least of all myself.

I asked Mark to leave. The children and I saw a movie while he packed his clothes. I continued to love him dearly, but courage gave me the strength to create a better atmosphere for my children and myself. The kids would know soon enough that their dad's love for me wasn't enough. I no longer wanted to be married to a secretive, conniving husband, who lied and lied and lied.

The night I made coffee, Dorothy took one look at the cup and commented, "My God! I have the same China pattern." Later, I sold the whole set to her soon-to-be ex-husband, when we met briefly to share our sorrow over losing our spouses. I never wanted to see them again. Dishes gone. No more sadness every time I saw them on the shelf.

Another excruciatingly painful day occurred before the divorce became final. As I drove to work one morning, I noticed Dorothy and Mark, who had started co-habitation when her husband slammed the door on her gorgeous behind. As they drove next to me on the highway, I could hardly keep the car on the road I shook so badly. My heart beat so fast, I thought I was having a heart attack. Not true. Just a broken heart.

When the divorce decree finalized, he took no pictures, no furniture except a large desk and left the house payment, car payment, the children and the challenges of a single parent on a limited income to me.

I'll give him credit. Although he saw the children irregularly, he never missed a support payment. I read the books stating not to denigrate the ex-spouse, which took strength and will power. As the children became adults, they realized his foibles, but he's their father. They love him, and I still wish that marriage had a happier ending.

The loss of my marriage caused me to think about the loss of my suitcase on my graduation adventure. Loss often leads to losing personal or emotional baggage. After the initial loss of my husband to another woman, I began to realize he was better baggage for her than for me.

Chapter 13

Baggage Gone; Dating On

Dating came in spurts. I dated a short, intelligent younger man, who didn't want a ready-made family. An older, boring lawyer, brought his favorite coffee cup for me to store in my kitchen for his use. His righteous, arrogant attitude rubbed me the wrong way. He was attractive, tall, and eloquent, but about ten years older. One night while at my house, he fell asleep during the after-dinner discussion of world events with a group of neighbors. We never dated after that. The man who called every night at 9:30, irritated me when I would miss the end of a television show. I'm still addicted to the 9:00 p.m. mystery shows, thirty years later.

I tried meeting Mr. Right by attending singles' groups, returning to sob into my pillow. With no relatives to assist, friends kept me sane. Looking back, my girlfriend, who would listen for hours, became a savior in my life. I never let men stay all night, although at times I missed the former closeness of the "baggage" I lost with my marriage.

I worked two part time jobs and as a full time school counselor when money became scarce. When I looked in the mirror, a stranger stared at me suffering from fatigue and worry. I rented the basement bedroom, which had a separate entrance, a few times to roomers. I enjoyed the extra cash.

When I needed a new vacuum, I worried about spending the money. The one I bought was a tan and aqua upright with a headlight. Both boys and I delighted in the purchase. The worry subsided as I watched the cash flow. Life became easier as I realized Mark's diligence in sending the checks and my ability to manage money.

When Joan Kennedy, whom I thought was Senator Ted Kennedy's ex-wife, came to Minneapolis to speak about her broken marriage, I found child care so that I could attend the event. I decided to attend her presentation to see how she managed her woes. Perhaps her story would cheer and inspire me. To my surprise, Joan Kennedy was not "the" Joan Kennedy. I stayed to hear her; she helped change my attitude with her amusing presentation resounding with a down-to-earth, spiritual message of hope.

Entertaining helped me evade the loneliness of single parenting. I invited guests to enjoy a forum for their thoughts at our Sunday Night Suppers. My boys helped me prepare the main dish and the others brought side dishes. Sometimes the boyfriend *du jour* attended, but most of the time the group involved friends, neighbors, or people who might be lonely.

The boys always had an opinion about each man in my life. They hated the handsome ex-convict, but loved the accountant with a lake house who took them fishing. Their intuition seemed razor sharp.

Mother insisted on my annual trip to Ohio, and she

arrived in Minneapolis every Christmas. She continued to harangue me about marrying "that man." She loved the boys, but lacked confidence caring for them. The kids loved her visits. She made their beds, which they recall fondly. She toted a bag full of gifts for "her boys," but she complained lustily about everything. I wanted to see her. I missed her from a distance and loved the letters she wrote from Ohio, but my blood pressure rose the moment she graced the front seat of the car. She raged about her fear of our dog and gerbil. She refused to learn how to use the microwave. The kids were too skinny. She thought Carl might have inherited my father's diabetic genes. Stress levels abated when I deposited her at the airport for her return trip home.

One night Grandma took charge while I ran a few errands. She suggested they find their sleeping bags to rest on the living room floor while she read a book. Carl put the gerbil in his sleeping bag. They fixed her! The gerbil made his appearance and disappeared, stuck or lost in the couch. Many days later his little beady eyes appeared, looking for food. Her agitation and anger make me laugh today, but on that night I wanted to cry. The boys considered themselves successful comedians that night.

Another day, when I telephoned from work to assure chaos was minimal, Carl faced danger. He caught a chipmunk in a paper bag and brought it to his bedroom for safekeeping. The chipmunk bit him as it fell through the bag and raced through the house. A trip to the doctor's office ensued. Thank goodness, Grandma had returned to Ohio the previous day. Both Carl and the chipmunk survived.

In 1981, I returned to Ohio for a high school graduation

reunion. The guy I dated in high school attended the party. We talked. We spent a little time together. Much to my surprise our roots and values aligned: his love of travel and the fact our families were friends all our lives helped forge the formidable task of a long-distance romance. We stayed in touch after he returned to Florida and I returned to Minnesota. My lengthy list of requirements encouraged me to stay in touch with him. He owned a van and a microwave. He lived in the South. He loved children, and my kids seemed to approve. Since he worked for a phone company he called me frequently. We visited each other several times. He wanted to marry, but I vacillated. Long discussions with my closest friend helped with decision making.

"You think I should pack up and go? How can I do that?"

"Why not rent your house while it's for sale?"

"In this economy, it might not sell for months."

"Hey! Do you love Ed?"

"Well, yeah. At least I think I do. The kids agree I should marry him."

"Kids often change their minds about step parents, but is he a drunk or wife beater?"

"What? I don't think so. I wish I could talk to his ex-wife to see what she'd say."

"Don't even go there. She'd say Ed mistreated her and good riddance. Didn't you say, she walked out on him and left him with a two-year-old and two older kids?"

"So you really think I should move?"

"Sure! You could stay here and keep dating. Or you could sell the snow-blower and your cross-country skis. You hate the cold weather and snow."

My silhouette reflected on the patio door as I trudged back and forth. I hesitated, made lists of attributes and liabilities, and created a cost analysis. I finally said, "I cannot imagine life without him."

One reason I waffled on the wedding was Ed's employment situation. He'd been laid off in Florida and had no job. His engineering skills and a diligent search helped him attract three job offers, all in Texas. When he accepted the job in Texas, relocation became inevitable.

The boys whined in harmony, "We don't want to leave our friends. We don't want to leave our school. We don't want you to marry him."

I bought a soft, cream-colored dress with a little lace on it. My girlfriend, the matron of honor, looked stunning in a dazzling pink dress. A neighbor played the role of Ed's best man, although they just met the night before we married. Another neighbor, a judge, married us in my home with the boys pretending to be happy and excited. The center of the wedding cake held a little pair of plastic cowboy boots. The script should have said, "Are you sure?" rather than "Two Steppin' to Texas."

Ed and I made a trip before the wedding to find and purchase a home big enough for a family of seven. We bought a four-bedroom ranch style home in a good school district. We married on Saturday, ready to travel to Texas on Monday. The suitcases, the moving van, and the car were packed for the long trip. The kids stayed with their father that weekend. Friends promised to correspond. The bittersweet road trip began, and the goldfish died in transit.

My kids decided that having a new dad was not such a

great idea. Step parenting landed in Dallas along with the boxes, suitcases, kids, and Scruffy, the dog, all part of the package deal.

It wasn't two steppin' to Texas. It was two million or maybe two trillion steps to Texas.

Chapter 14

Two Stepping into Texas

"How's come they got the front bedrooms? I wanted that room!"

Thus began the next thirty years of my life. The saying over the door of the church in Chambon says to "Love One Another." We loved each other in our family, but issues began erupting like popcorn in a popper. The dance became easier over the years, but never ended.

We arrived in Texas the Tuesday after we married. His children stayed temporarily with his ex-wife. As we created a new life for this motley bunch, we struggled. Step parenting is like our HVAC system: it blows hot and cold, occasionally needing repair, but when it works, it's wonderful.

After his children arrived from Florida, my ten-year-old and thirteen-year-old fought bravely to stay in the room where twin beds and their clothing covered the floor. Ed's two sons were the youngest age and oldest of the group, aged five and fifteen. They would stay in the bedroom next to my boys. Skye, the only girl, also thirteen, hated the fourth bedroom. Loud voices, tears and arguments resounded throughout the house. Why couldn't they choose their bedrooms? The tip of the iceberg showed, despite the balmy Texas weather. The iceberg had a neon sign on top saying, "Ed likes his kids best." Another sign on the iceberg read, "Ruth, you play favorites."

Our "unblended" family consisted of…

Nick, the oldest, complained about Texas immediately. His friends and mom wanted him in Florida. He was angry, belligerent, and hateful. Big for his age, a little pudgy with acne and an attitude, he didn't like the new, bigger school. The teachers picked on him and made fun of his accent, so he said.

Bill, my older son, knew his status appeared low on the totem pole in the family. He hid behind books, finding solace in his volunteer job at a nearby used book store. He stayed out of the minefields in our new home.

Skye pranced around, not quite realizing she no longer held the role of female head of the household. Her *raison d'être* appeared to be a leading lady, regardless of the circumstances. But, she seemed happy to have a "new" mom, who bought her cute, stylish clothes, rather than jeans from Sears. At thirteen, she wanted make-up, many friends, trendy clothes, and I had a daughter. I was elated and ready, so I thought.

Carl, my younger son, faded into the background with his curly, brown hair and a quick smile. He found friends quickly in the neighborhood. I thought he was adjusting. Little did I realize the depth of his emotions, until he came to me one day, asking when he could meet with Ed and me.

"Mom, when do I get to meet with you and Ed?"

"What do you mean, Carl?"

"You're always talking with Nick. When do I get to talk with you and Ed?"

Unpredictable problems arose with Nick. The dinner table offered time for family discussions. All of us attended counseling. Nick lived in the center of many disagreements. He didn't want to wear deodorant. He didn't want to take baths. Maybe depression? Probably all of us found this union depressing. I would stand at the window with tears running down my face, *Why do I feel so sad? This is what I want. I made this decision. God, please help me cope.*

Harry, the youngest—stocky with a charming smile—created volatile challenges for me, challenges for which I was unprepared.

He walked like his dad, looked like his dad and his older brother, both with deep brown eyes and brown hair. Ed is a red-head with green eyes, but they all three walked with a swagger. I cannot tell the difference in their voices on the telephone, now that Harry's grown. Their interests in cars and technology last to this day.

I still thought loving all of them would suffice.

We spent an incredible amount of time herding the kids to soccer games and other sports events, trying to meld the family into a cohesive family. Never happened. I felt I could certainly handle any misgivings others had. I was wrong.

We plodded through the issues. Harry was Ed's favorite. Ed carried him around similar to a kangaroo mother. Finally, I asked, "Does he have something wrong with his legs?"

Father and son liked the arrangement. Ed felt sorry for Harry, as Harry's mom abandoned the family when Harry was two, leaving Ed to manage single parenting. Harry's anger showed repeatedly, when he would shout at me, "I don't have to do what you say. You're not my mom."

I wondered how love would conquer all. My role certainly seemed like "the evil step mother" with characters in my home straight out of *Snow White and the Seven Dwarfs*. However, I had only one little dwarf and four big ones, plus a new husband who wanted peace, not World War III.

We found a church home after all seven of us trooped into thirteen different churches. Ed attended a Baptist church in Florida, and I attended a less conservative denomination in Minnesota.

I couldn't do "Baptist." Just too rigid and conservative for me. Out of the thirteen churches we visited, we left two before the service. No music in one. My parents were musicians. How could I attend a church with no hymns? I passed the word down the row of our family members. All of us rose simultaneously and trooped to the van in a long line, like ducks. The children, happy to leave the droning preacher, looked puzzled and amused. In the second church we departed, I gave the command to leave when the minister blasted the Catholics in his sermon. Our church visitations gave us a chance to discuss our beliefs and understand why I wanted our family to depart church on those memorable days. How could we attend a church where the minister chastised Catholics? I couldn't. We couldn't. I wanted to find a church that epitomized what I learned in Chambon.

A good youth program in any church remained high on my list of priorities for the children. When we attended one of the local Methodist churches more than once, the kids decided to attend Sunday School to assess the possibility of a new church home. The second Sunday at this church, Bill (my older son) wanted to return in the evening for the youth program. Actually, he probably saw a pretty girl who smiled at him, who piqued his curiosity.

People in our Sunday School class came from many faiths. The Indian wife of one man worked for a minister in another denomination. Several Catholics, Baptists and Jewish people in the class became our circle of friends. We loved the choir, the people, the music and the ministers. The hymns we sang reminded me of the ones from my childhood. The minister's sermons supplied strength for everyday living. When Ed and I were invited to a social gathering in the new church, we recognized the kindness and support from their members.

The earth stopped shaking so badly, but serious issues kept creeping into view. The lessons and comments in the Sunday School class helped us realize most families, if they are honest, must deal with a fair amount of dysfunction. When we heard their stories, our worries lessened.

We traveled with the kids, hoping to instill and inspire them to learn about the history and culture through on-site experiences. We found joy off the beaten tracks and in big cities with them before they became adults.

Dancing the "two-step" demanded more than cowboy boots. The floor had splinters with uneven boards, yet the two of us continued the dance to learn new steps to keep moving forward.

Chapter 15

Coping

Nick, Ed's oldest son, continued to succumb to a bad attitude. He found a lawyer to support his effort to return to Florida. When Nick was fifteen, the State of Texas allowed him to decide where he wanted to live, if his mom agreed. He left the family about a year after we married. Quite frankly, the situation became far more tolerable with no more fists through the wall, chairs thrown and teenage temper tantrums.

Ed was devastated, but Nick did not want to follow our house rules. When Nick left, a part of Ed died. Big guys, tough guys, good hearts. Their love of the outdoors, including camping and hunting, would need to wait. Shouting and hateful words led to a sad departure.

A year later, Nick's twelve-year-old cousin shot him in a freak hunting accident. Nick lay dying in a faraway hospital. Emotionally and rationally, we decided I should stay with the kids, and Ed would fly to Florida for the inevitable. Nick lived three days, the longest three days of my life.

My mother's health and demeanor deteriorated. When

she demolished her car near her home, she thought she had gone to sleep at the wheel, but the doctors said she experienced a TIA or a mini-stroke. She needed to downsize. I asked her to move to Texas, but she refused.

"My life is here. I'm still teaching music, and my friends live here. Never. I will never move to Texas."

"But, Mother, I find it difficult to see you with all my responsibilities and the kids' issues. My business and the family issues make it incredibly difficult to visit."

Soon after Nick left, I started my own consulting business. While in Minnesota, I had worked in several schools as a counselor. Two of my jobs entailed placing at-risk students into jobs. My counseling service morphed into a recruiting and outplacement company over the years after our arrival in Dallas. I thought placing adults would be as easy as placing students. Having my own company helped with flexibility in my life, but came with a steep learning curve. I loved my new career, although the challenges of accounting and selling while teaching people how to find jobs added stress to the family versus business equity. Would I rather feel guilty about my family or guilty I had not called the client as regularly as I wanted? Family issues took priority since I owned the company.

Three years later, as my mom, still in Ohio, arranged to sell her home and move to an apartment, the doctor informed me I had breast cancer. More decision-making. I certainly had no solid answers. Should I delay surgery?

"Doc, I can't have this surgery right now. My mother needs me. I need to be with her. Ed can care for the kids while I help her sell her home and move to a smaller place.

She's so alone. She's planning for an auction next weekend. And there's the business. . ."

"Now you listen to me. If you were my wife, you'd have this operation tomorrow. The mass is large. If you want to be around for those kids, you'll have the operation this week." The dark journey fell at the feet of spiritual and medical guidance. I trusted the doctor, and knew my mother's faith and friends would provide the needed support for her.

I called my mother with the news, and I explained to the children and Ed that I would need their love and support. Facing cancer with considerable family chaos and a business to manage shaped a difficult triangle. We knew about grief from Nick's death, but I didn't expect the gamut of individualized emotions from the family. The boys asked a few pertinent questions and decided "no problem."

Ed's mother died at fifty-two from cancer. The terror of cancer created fear in his world. Faith and family somehow managed to help him focus on the "little things" like getting food on the table, helping with the kids' homework, and hugging his daughter as often as possible. But our life strayed far from peaceful.

Perhaps Skye thought she would lose another mother as she needed many daddy hugs. She was sixteen, the age when daughters begin to move away from family values. I became the wicked step mother in her life. Typical teenage behavior, but difficult to swallow while recuperating from cancer surgery. Skye's behavior seemed normal: her room looked as if a bomb exploded. Clean clothes, mixed with dirty jeans, half full glasses with green moss on them didn't faze her, yet I wanted a clean house. I was grumpy, I'm sure.

Skye found happiness with her friends, despite her step mother's interference. She increased her activity in Thespians where she participated in acting and production work. Beautiful, with long golden brown hair and a quick smile, Skye's outgoing personality kept her busy with friends. She excelled in volleyball, gymnastics, and other sports. We were proud of her acting ability on the stage, but not at home. Friends, more boys than girls, surrounded Skye at school. I never worried about drinking, driving or drugs, but her attitude often made me wince with emotional pain.

Toleration played a role in our home. Since Bill attended the same high school, he and Skye avoided taking the same classes. Their friends moved in different circles. We coped, but we didn't blend.

Skye's hostility lasted far longer than I expected. Ed stayed lodged between the proverbial "rock and a hard place," as he didn't want to lose another child to his ex-wife. I understood her resentment, but I cried myself to sleep many nights.

The event I recall most vividly happened when my mother came to visit. Skye, with a little prodding, graciously gave her room to Grandma. She slept on the couch in the family room. Skye was dating a nice sixteen-year-old boy, who came from a nice family and lived in a nice house. We approved of his nice manners. One night during Grandma's visit, Grandma thought a robber tried to break through Skye's window. I heard her shout, "Ruth, Ruth, Ruth!" Her bark sounded like a scared dog. I rushed to see what ailed my skinny, elderly mother. Rocks hit the window, scaring her far more than moving to Texas.

"Someone's trying to get in the window."

Ed sneaked outside and captured Skye's boyfriend. It was 3:00 a.m. We called his parents, who voiced anger for being disturbed. Yes, he'd stolen their car. Yes, send him home. And Skye was furious! We chose not to call the cops.

We muddled through the teenage years, making mistakes but trying hard to be fair. Skye, Bill and Carl graduated and went to college. Ed and I became closer. Harry hated high school, dropped out and went to work. Although Ed and I tried to convince him to stay in school, Harry spent the next few years working in dead-end jobs before he decided to finish his high school education. Harry turned his life around when he met a wonderful, wild, and wise woman who captured his heart at age twenty.

Church always played an important role in our lives. My business kept me challenged and eager to face each day. Happiness revolved around work, church, friends, and the family. Grandchildren appeared—the smartest, cutest and most wonderful youngsters on the planet. Ed and I began to travel more, especially to see the youngsters.

Ed retired in 2001. He's happy with periodic, part time jobs and loves his hobby of photography. Two summers he worked at Yellowstone National Park. I stayed home with the dog, busy with my consulting. With my flexible self-employment opportunities and his retirement, international travel became possible in the new century.

Part Three

A Passion for Travel

Chapter 16

Tripping in Paris

The kids became adults. Our travel without children began with a round trip ticket to Paris. Someone who worked with Ed suggested Hotel Regyn-Montmartre near *Sacré Coeur* (Sacred Heart) Cathedral. From the airport, we found a cab and managed to arrive at the tiny, boutique hotel. The Abbesses Metro subway stop near the hotel helped us travel throughout the city. We laughed about the size of the hotel elevator. Fitting two suitcases, two backpacks and two adults in it? No way.

The lively area bustled with neighborhood activity with the local residents purchasing loaves of bread and pastries from the shops. As we wandered through the neighborhood or sat in the little park near the hotel, we were part of the microcosm. An old man swilled from his bottle in a paper bag and kids shouted with joy. Moms and nannies watched their little ones at play. We observed a delightful marriage ceremony across the street at *St. Jean de Montmartre* Church from our hotel window without anyone's notice. A well-dressed mother and child exited during the ceremony to allow the little boy to pee on a bush by the church.

Our friend gave us good advice about the hotel. The dust balls danced under our bed, but they did not bother us. The location provided exceptional walking tours. The view at night allowed us to gaze at the glowing Eiffel tower from our far-away advantage on the hill. Ed set the clock for 3:00 early one morning to capture the illuminated beauty with his camera. His magnificent picture adorns a wall in our dining room to remind us of the fun we had near *Sacré Coeur* Cathedral and *Le Moulin Rouge*. A short walk up the hill towards the church beckoned us to rest in a small square called *Place de Tertre,* a famous location for artists and tourists. I recognized it as the location of one of the four prints I purchased long ago on my first trip to France.

We explored other parts of the city, walking under the *Arche de Triomphe*, holding hands, buying a *sandwich de fromage* (cheese) along the way. I bought key chains with miniature Eiffel Tower fobs to pack for gifts. My neck grew longer as I stretched to view the top of the Eiffel Tower from underneath its base.

The *Musée du Louvre* brought back memories from my first trip when I ran down the long corridors to lose the so-called thug who chased me around town. On this visit, both Ed and I wanted to stay longer. The statues, the artifacts, and the marble floors kept me in awe of the good fortune to be in Paris again after decades, this time with my loved one.

One night as we walked back to the hotel from a *prix fixe* dinner of pecan-crusted salmon and glorious red wine, we heard a male voice close behind. Turning around, we saw an elegantly groomed, tall lady, dressed flamboyantly. His/her red satin dress, fruit-flavored cologne, and cigar held with matching red nails assailed our senses. S/he beckoned Ed to come with him/her. "*Non, merci,*" worked perfectly.

We purchased tickets to Giverny, where Monet lived from 1883 until his death in 1926. The train took us to Vernon, where a tour bus awaited its passengers. The tulips, blooming gloriously, thrilled us as we arrived. Ed shot a fabulous photo of the lilies in the pond and bridge in Monet's famous painting, which is often shown in travel advertisements. The large garden of tulips allowed tourists to wander the pathways for closer looks at sizes and colors: red, orange, pink, yellow, cerise, lavender, and deep purple, all superbly planted in row after colorful row.

The tour buses started leaving for the train in Vernon. Unfortunately, our slow progress through the garden kept us from visiting inside Monet's home. No disappointment for us, because capturing photos of the flowers and garden sufficed.

To our dismay, the trains went on strike (*la grêve*) while we had wandered across the bridge over the lily pads. The last tourist bus took us to Vernon, where we would board the train to return to Paris. When we arrived, people stood by the track, hoping for one more train to rumble into the station, despite the strike. We crossed the street to the neighborhood bar, joining the other tourists for *un vin* (wine) or *une bière* (beer). The swarthy barman did the common put-nose-in-air-and-make-a-nose-noise, when asked about the next train. I had no difficulty understanding that "Maybe a train would come later and maybe not."

Several people in the bar, alarmed about how we would find our way to our hotels, decided to hire a vociferous, French imbiber to drive us to Paris. With his claim that he used to drive a taxi in Paris four of us decided to give our life savings for a ride to our hotels. Just as we began climbing into his car, we heard a whistle in the distance. By the time the train came screaming to a quick halt, we were able to hop out of the rusty, beat-up, four-door Citroen and rush to the wooden staging area for the train. The drunk returned our money before we sprinted to the train, adding another surprise for our day. Luck rode with us. The train carried us safely without the drunken Frenchman weaving his way to Paris.

Several years later, my shouts of happiness could be heard from Dallas to Houston. My son Bill would be an ex-patriate in Europe to expand his company's software business for two years: one year in Paris, then moving to London for his second year. Ed and I decided to visit Paris and London with a place to stay both years. We planned to spend time with Bill for a few days and make a quick trip to Zurich via train for a long weekend.

Bill lived in the Sixteenth Arrondissement (rather like our zip code districts), abundantly blessed with fabulous coffee shops, small restaurants, and retail shops. After Bill left for work, we dodged the dog poop on the sidewalks strolling to the nearby bar for coffee and croissants. The neighborhood came alive with the merchants opening their shops and workers hustling to the Metro. After our first visit to the nearby coffee bar, the barman recognized Ed and me, immediately bringing us our morning *café au lait et deux croissants au chocolat.*

Tripping in Paris

Bill's apartment, a hodge-podge of used furniture, charmed us. A small garden behind the building needed a little weeding, but offered a quiet respite from the Paris hubbub. The eclectic décor delivered atmosphere in a real neighborhood. The retro lamps produced dim light but enhanced the Parisian feel. The lime green walls, an uncomfortable art deco couch and chair, the purple lamp shade on the floor lamp created the perfect apartment for a single guy.

The narrow stairwell to the loft, where we planned to sleep, proved problematic. Since my middle name could be "Klutz," I tumbled, not too gracefully, half-way down the steep steps. My arm and back hurt. I could hardly walk on the left leg. Pain grabbed my ankle and would not let go. I watched my leg starting to turn green and purple. Would I need to go to the hospital? Which bone did I break?

"Mom, nothing is broken. You'll be fine tomorrow!"

"Now, Ruth, you put your leg up. Bill, do you have any ice?"

"I'm sure it's broken. I remember when I fell at Toastmasters Club a few years ago. It wasn't broken, but I wore a cast for six weeks. Is there a hospital nearby?"

"Mom, let's wait until tomorrow morning to see how you feel."

"Ok. But where's the nearest emergency room?"

"Mom, it's not broken!" His voice rose significantly.

I dragged my poor swollen leg behind me to the loft for the night. In the morning, the leg remained a little swollen, but Bill was correct. It wasn't broken.

"Is there a pharmacy nearby? I need an ace bandage."

I hobbled with Bill to the pharmacy to help translate for the pharmacist. My tall, lanky, blond son walked too fast, of course. Nice guy with a Charlie Chan moustache at the pharmacy fixed me right up.

We said good-bye to Bill on Friday morning, dragging my leg and suitcase with me to go to the train station for our trek to Zurich. When we arrived, another surprise awaited, another *grève* (strike). I recognized the "nose-in-the-air-spssst" sound at the ticket office. "Madam, the trains will not run this weekend."

Not only were the trains on strike, but also a sanitation strike affected the beauty of Paris. The piles and piles of rotting food and other waste created a stench in the streets and train depot. We made a quick decision.

Why not take a bus tour to see more of France? My leg didn't hurt too badly as we walked near the Louvre. Tourist offices and tour buses abound in that area. Sometimes miserable situations morph into delight.

We found a tour that took us to see *Mont Saint Michel* and several other castles. Saint Michel captured my heart forever.

If I could choose the "wonders of the world," Mont Saint Michel would be on my list. On the tour, the guide told us the peasants began building the structure for the Benedictine monks in 966 A.D. We marveled at the size of the rocks to the top of the steep, stony island surrounded by water during high tide. Every six hours, high tide encircles the tall stone chapel upon the rocks. Low tide allows for a sandy beach to reach the miracle of the structure by road (most of the time). Tourists arrive all months of the year, regardless of inclement weather. The tides become much higher with the full moon.

The steps to the top are steep and difficult to ascend, especially with a bum leg. I dragged my encased leg through the eerily echoing rooms of the castle, stopping periodically to rest. Ed struggled more than I did, huffing and puffing like a tea kettle about to whistle. The guide provided fascinating facts about *St. Michel*, whose statue sits proudly on top to guard and guide good and evil, the way God intends.

Standing in the middle of an ancient dining room in the castle, I said a short prayer of thanksgiving, as I knew this was a bit of Heaven on Earth. The wonderful guide and unexpected tour created an unplanned, but happy adventure. How fortunate to hear the stories of this amazing structure, built long before America was discovered.

When we returned to Paris, we made time for one last museum, *Musée de l'Orangerie*. Monet's "Water Lilies" encircle visitors with tight security. I didn't see the sign that said, "Don't sit on the little edge which surrounds the 360 degree presentation of the painting." A buzzer sounded and the guard rushed towards me to assure no damage or theft was in process. Take it from me. Don't try it.

Zurich remains for another trip.

Chapter 17

The Phantom in Our Family

As planned, we packed for Europe the next fall. Bill and Tiffany, his long-term girlfriend, had married and moved to London. Anticipation grew with each minute. My new daughter-in-law purchased tickets for all of us to attend *Phantom of the Opera*, my all-time favorite show. Tiffany's quiet graciousness radiated throughout the visit.

Tall, elegant, quiet Tiffany accompanied us to several museums and Harrod's Department store, while Bill worked. We wove through the antique stores around Portobello, where I stopped to buy a strange, little, wooden turquoise bird with wire legs. I remember the tasty pizza we ate along a narrow street on a gray day. Despite her shy, reserved manner, she coped confidently with her in-laws. We enjoyed the day exploring the winding streets with exquisite architecture.

Their tiny two-bedroom walk-up made me smile. Turning around in the bathroom was almost impossible. The shower would be small for a Chihuahua, and the kitchen had no space for a table. We ate most of our meals nearby, walking, as all Londoners do. I recall disappointment in Ed's eyes, when they chose a sushi bar. He hates Japanese food, but managed to gulp a few bites, like a minnow. Afterwards, we ditched Bill and Tiffany to find a fish and chips joint. Ed didn't go hungry that night before returning to the "wee box."

As we sat in the second row at the theater for *Phantom*, my mind wandered to what the future of my son and his wife would bring, with no inkling of later sadness in their lives. With the kettle drums booming and the music ringing in my ears, I prayed for wisdom and joy for the handsome couple in their tiny London apartment.

Before we left Texas for London, we planned to take the train from London to Dunbar and then to nearby Edinburgh. I chose this little town because long ago a branch of the family tree held a few Dunbars. The small, seaside town on the west coast offered a chance to view the ocean churning from the high cliffs by Dunbar Castle. I imagined meeting the people in the town and getting acquainted with the owner of the bed and breakfast. The next stop would be Edinburgh.

When I researched Dunbar, I found that it was John Muir's birthplace. I'd been to Muir Beach in California and knew his fame for his conservation efforts. Dunbar offered the chance to see a "real" Scottish town. I don't recall the name of the B&B I chose from the Internet, but I knew we'd find it charming and maybe I would find a relative hiding in the closet.

Shortly before we left the apartment for Dunbar and Edinburgh, a train derailed close to our destination. No longer would we arrive quickly, but the intended train for our trip would stop about every fifty feet to drop off or take on new passengers. We debated whether to continue.

The adventure began. Much of the time, we sat between cars on a type of "rumble seat" with a new definition for uncomfortable. It was a round, metal disk, pulled down from the wall beside a small window in the door to see the countryside. I loved watching the sheep in the mottled, green fields. Fewer goats were evident, yet I felt like singing "The Sound of Music" or at least a few bars from *Phantom of the Opera*. I don't think the young Scot sitting across from me on his yellow, iron disk would have appreciated my off-key renditions. He had visited his mother in London and was returning to a small college where he majored in computer science. Talkative and pleasant, his commentary about the scenery helped the hours fly. Ed watched the scenery and people while the college kid and I chatted until our stop at Dunbar. When the petite lady with the loud voice and a big suitcase departed the train, we could maneuver more easily in the cramped space.

We shivered like icicles in a bad storm traipsing from the train stop in Dunbar to our B&B. The winds came bursting over us, almost knocking us to the ground. The innkeeper gave us extra blankets, yet I wondered if any heat came through the vents. Dinner consisted of tepid soup with a plate of beans and pork chops resembling hockey pucks, but we were famished and thankful for the food. Lights in the pub across the street burned brightly but fatigue and the weather prevented us from finding more excitement. We snuggled against each other in the uncomfortable bed, hoping morning would come quickly. Our twelve-hour day brought slumber immediately, and then the sun rose too soon, peeping through the clouds into our bedroom window.

The innkeeper pounded on the door with his fat fist, telling us to dash to the train station if we wanted to arrive in Edinburgh that day. We made it, dragging the suitcases in the gusty, misty, miserable weather. No time for tea or breakfast that morning.

The twelve-hour trip on the train delivered much more than sore backs from the uncomfortable seats. The discussion with the college guy and the chance to see Scotland's vast fields are fond memories about the kindness everyone on the train reflected with no unruly or disruptive people, despite the discomfort and slow progress to our destinations.

We arrived in Edinburgh with one site on our "must see" list. Queen Elizabeth's yacht was moored close to the city. We donned our warmest clothes to wander through the ship, which the Queen used to entertain dignitaries, family and friends from 1953-1997. I could almost hear the tinkling Baccarat stemmed glasses and imagine the royal dishes and silver arranged for an elegant night of entertaining. The wind blew in icy gusts as we walked on the bow of the boat.

We wandered up the steep hill to the Edinburgh Castle where the view offered a chance to see the numerous churches and museums from a distance. History claims a castle has existed on the site since the Twelfth Century. From the castle, we walked to a tea shop where it appears that Sir Arthur Conan Doyle may have written his novels while sipping his hot drink with milk. The tea shop bustled with people who stopped to warm themselves and have a pastry. Our waitress had no time to explain its history. We had time to visit a few retail shops where the genteel clerks assisted me in purchasing a few woolen items for gifts.

Life is full of surprises. Ed and I stayed on track, even when the other train derailed. Seeing the countryside at a slow pace and hearing the stories of people on the way created a more colorful, memorable trip.

Sadly, Tiffany died six years later, in surgery from a raging blood disease, leaving Bill with a four-year-old autistic son and a five-year-old daughter. *Phantom of the Opera* fosters sadness whenever I hear the soundtrack. Life will never be the same without Tiffany.

Chapter 18

Planning the Pilgrimage

One of my recruiting assignments kept me in the car two hours a day with ten-hour days on site. The job paid well and I liked the people and technology, but my exhaustion led to pneumonia. Life wasn't much fun. Those long hours driving along the freeways, in the dark both ways, pushed me into serious soul-searching. I quit after five months, but stayed until I found a suitable replacement.

"Isn't it time for another trip?" I questioned the loved one, once I recuperated.

"Where shall we go this time?"

"We haven't been to Italy. That's on my bucket list."

"You know, we've never taken a tour. We would visit many places in a short time, but not with much depth."

"I'm not sure I want to travel with the same people for a week or ten days. We might tire of the group. What about the dog?"

"Why not plan to tour for a week and then go to that place in France where you worked?"

"Might be fascinating. I wonder whatever happened to

Marie, the exchange student who connected me with her mom in Chambon."

A friend suggested a travel agent who helped me plan the trip. The agent, very cordial and professional, told us not to cover too much territory due to geographic realities. With Italy's extensive history and geography, we needed to decide whether to take the northern route, which included Venice, or the southern tour, which included Sicily. No problem with that decision, as I yearned to see Venice, the lake country, plus Rome and Florence. Since I had started collecting glass paperweights, I knew we'd visit Murano, near Venice, where spectacular paperweights and art glass are crafted.

"Listen!" the loved one said. "Let's stay another week to visit that place you've told me about."

"You mean le Chambon-sur-Lignon? I'm not sure. I don't want to be gone longer than two weeks."

"Ah, c'mon! It would be quite an adventure. You've talked about the town and people throughout the years. The town left its mark on you. Let's call it a pilgrimage."

Rather than continuing to beat myself up, I listened to my body and my husband. Truthfully, thinking about Chambon increased my enthusiasm to revisit the small town.

I researched travel from Rome to Chambon, discovering divine stopping points: Nice and Avignon dotted the railroad stops on the map to reach Lyon before the final destination of Chambon. The trip percolated. I had wanted to visit Avignon since my friends in Chambon and I sang about the bridge over the river in the ancient city. What a wonderful opportunity to visit the *Palais des Papes* (Palace of the Popes) and taste the food of Provence. Gaily, I sang the little folk song about the bridge in Avignon over and over.

"Sur le Pont, d'Avignon,
L'on y danse, L'on y danse.
Sur le Pont, d'Avignon,
L'on y danse, Toute en ronde."

During a conversation with a close friend, she revealed insight about Chambon. She read a book telling the story of the five thousand Jewish children saved by the townspeople. She recommended I locate a film she saw during her religious studies to become a Presbyterian minister. Pierre Sauvage produced a video about Chambon during World War II.

Sauvage was born and lived in Chambon with his parents during the war, coming to America at age four. His parents rarely mentioned the history of Chambon and failed to tell him he was Jewish (which he discovered at age eighteen). When he visited the town in his early twenties, he realized the vast importance that its history holds. His life is dedicated to producing documentaries about saving the Jews.

I began to delve into the history with new eyes and ears for the significance of Chambon, not just in my lifetime. Although the people of Chambon treated me as "one of them," I failed to realize the magnitude of fear and risk the *Chambonais* (people from Chambon) experienced during World War II when they saved Jewish children and adults.

Authors and residents quibble over exact numbers of people and children saved, because recording numbers during the period would have been foolhardy. History books from 1939 to1945 decry the six million Jews who died in concentration camps or the gas ovens, an undeniable human travesty. Although the exact number cannot be documented, we know Chambon became a safe haven for those in jeopardy during the war.

Finding the film *Weapons of the Spirit,* the video by Sauvage, frustrated me, as it wasn't readily available. Then, I discovered a copy right in my backyard. Southern Methodist University stores a copy in its Dallas library. Ed decided to accompany me on the sixty-mile round trip to SMU. No one can borrow the CD, but interested people can watch it in the college computer lab. I gasped as I watched it three times, taking copious notes.

The producer's voice prefaced vignettes of various people who lived through those troubled times. The parents of Marie, the exchange student, who told me about Chambon, spoke of their challenges in the 1940s in the production. Her mom looked almost the same as when she delivered me to the rest home where I worked the year I graduated from Ohio State. In the film, Marie's parents look like people in the painting, "The Gleaners" by Camille Pissarro. Stoic, hardworking, always helping others.

I skimmed several books, but the film told the story succinctly. We decided to visit this little tourist town to see how it might have changed. Looking back, I realize skimming was a mistake; I should have digested every word. I continued to miss the gravity of the story. Pierre Sauvage's film, *Weapons of the Spirit*, was produced in 1991, before the adults who cared for the children began to die of old age. Integrating the information before the trip increased my enthusiasm.

Our Italian tour would start in Rome, ramble through Tuscany, stop in Venice before ending in Florence by bus. I could smell the garlic and visualize sitting in a coffee shop in Rome.

After the Italian tour, we would take the train from Florence to Milan, switch to another train and stay the night in Nice. We picked a few sites to explore in Nice before we boarded the train. Travel along the Mediterranean Coast would allow us to watch the beauty along the way. Granted, much of the territory would flash by our train windows, but Ed and I agreed trains work for us. Excitement grew. Friends questioned our sanity about taking the train rather than flying to Lyon, but we both wanted to gaze at the azure water with shifting sailboats and massive cliffs along the Mediterranean.

We planned to arrive in Avignon in the evening to stay two nights, allowing a full day of sight-seeing in Avignon, and another night in Lyon before beginning our pilgrimage to Chambon. From Lyon, we would take another train to St. Étienne and a bus to Chambon. No trains ran directly to Chambon in 2006. Chambon offered a treat Americans tourists rarely see.

No other way, other than driving, would work. Since Ed and I tend to argue with each other regarding directions when we travel by car, we stick to trains and planes, rather than road trips in foreign countries. Coordination took many hours, but the investment paid dividends.

I made a second trip to Southern Methodist University to view the video since I found many books too detailed for a quick review. The desk clerk recognized me on my second visit. The university library lab seemed cold and bleak, although the campus is historic and handsome with big, gray buildings, bustling with students and professors. The desk clerk registered disinterest in my discoveries about the tiny French town, despite my zeal. I kept asking myself, *Why doesn't the world know about the five thousand Jewish children saved by the people of Chambon during the war?*

Packing the suitcases entailed planning a wardrobe for several seasons. Weather might be tricky with distance and time. Our trip in Italy would require quick-dry clothes and a willingness to wear two pairs of jeans for two weeks without a washing machine. What if we lost our suitcases? History might repeat itself. What if we missed our train connections? Who would keep the dog? With more questions than answers, we moved forward with determination to reach our destinations. My heart churned with anticipation.

More research helped me gain new perspective with the Internet at hand. Andre Trocmé started the school, the same school where I audited the French as a second language class. Trocmé demonstrated foresight that the war would advance into Southern and Central France. With a strong message to the Huguenot residents about upcoming challenges, his faith gave him courage to face the upcoming upheaval. He assembled a strong leadership team to support the resistance efforts. Trocmé established *Le Collège* for a safe haven for Jewish children. Teachers, both Jews and non-Jews, arrived with the purpose to educate rather than be marched off to prison camps, or worse, because of their views. The community rose to challenge evil in the world.

Most residents in the small town with less than three thousand residents shared the responsibility of housing and educating the children who began pouring into the town on the little train, mostly between 1939 and 1943.

The children and other newcomers undoubtedly rode the same train I rode on that sunny, scary day when I arrived with no job and two outfits to wear. Their fears were far greater than mine.

Most of France is Catholic, but Chambon-sur-Lignon is largely Huguenot, the pre-cursor of the Presbyterian and Reformed Church denominations. Their persecution over many centuries is well-documented in history. History books offer details of the atrocities against their ancestors. The people of Chambon willingly hid the Jewish children when the police and military searched their homes. They followed Trocmé's passion for peace by treating all people with love. Trocmé understood the agony and horror parents suffered when they put their children on the trains for uncertain futures.

History seems destined to repeat itself with little awareness of past atrocities. With the raging angst in the world today, we need to re-visit how the war evolved, how the Jews were mistreated, how their jobs became politicized and forbidden simply because of ethnicity. They could no longer support their families or they might be shot. Their homes were pillaged and looted, with nothing left but to send their children to a tiny town in Central France where they hoped their children would be safe. And they were.

Trocmé home in Chambon

Trocmé's wife played a key role in assigning the children to locations as they arrived on the little train or sometimes on foot. Some stayed in the numerous dormitories, supported by philanthropic organizations. Some were documented, staying a few months or longer, hoping their parents would come to take them to other, safer countries. Many children never saw their parents again. Some were smuggled by train or under the cover of night into neutral Switzerland, ducking under barbed-wire barricades. They arrived in small groups in Chambon or two-by-two or with a note pinned inside a shabby coat or secretly tucked inside a *filet* (rope bag) with a small sandwich.

The war brought rationing for everyone. Central France

suffered lack of food. Shoes became rationed to one pair a year. Finding food, clothing, and hiding places kept the little town of Chambon scurrying to find "another potato for the pot."

One of the saddest stories I read about the life during the war talked about Daniel Trocmé, Andre's cousin, reportedly an atheist. He managed one of the dormitories for the teenagers. Roundups occurred when the police, Gestapo, or the French Army would search a home or institution for people "with long noses." Daniel's dormitory, called "House of Rocks," became the target of fourteen armed marauders. No one knows for sure whether they were Gestapo or military police, but they traveled a distance to find "the Jews." Not all the children were Jewish. Some were German, others French, Austrian, Polish and other nationalities, sent by families for the security offered in Chambon.

The incident in Daniel's dorm happened in 1943 as the war escalated. In the past many of the "enemy" overlooked the reality of the large number of students and young children in Chambon. The Gestapo took all seventeen or eighteen students away from Chambon. Daniel went with the children because he thought himself safe with his reputation as a non-believer. Although Madame Trocmé cooked a hearty meal for the evil intruders, they loaded the children and Daniel into military vehicles for the trip. According to one author, only seven of the eighteen were Jewish. They went to a prison camps; several never reappeared. Daniel never returned. Clearly, roundups were the beginning of the end of five years of hiding the children.

We packed our suitcases and flew to Rome to meet

our tour guide for our Italian holiday. Thoughts rushed through my head about Italy. I pictured myself wandering through the Colosseum, looking for Daniel and the lions. The research and study of Italy and Central France created additional excitement and comprehension for the upcoming trip.

Chapter 19

Morris and Max

Our suitcases weighed more than usual as we prepared for weather conditions on the trip. We would need jackets. Italy would be sunny, but France might be chilly. Hadn't I learned to travel light, a lesson long ago when I lost my suitcase on the way to France the first time? My ugly, dark green nylon jacket took too much space in my suitcase, but once we arrived in Chambon, I appreciated the value of carrying the noisy, slick garment for the damp, dreary weather we encountered.

A travel company representative met us at the airport in Italy with a limo and wild ride to the nearby hotel outside Rome. We met our guide in the hotel lobby that evening. The elaborate works of art, the scenery, and the historic buildings were more magnificent than the tour books portrayed. When a few hiccups happened on the trip, I realized tours depend on the competence of the guide, not necessarily the tour company.

Our guide shared tidbits of history, such as when Bernini wanted bronze for part of St. Peter's Basilica, he

Inside the Vatican

took it from the Pantheon's roof. Today Italians spend more taxes on building roads than on restoring and maintaining their historical edifices.

Rome, glorious, colorful Rome. We stayed outside the city, riding a big bus into the city to see sites like the Pantheon, the Coliseum, the famous churches with their mosaics, statues, and paintings. When I saw the Roman Colosseum, I didn't find any lions, but I visualized the gladiators with horses pounding their hooves into the dirt. The Trevi Fountain? I hummed "Three Coins in the Fountain." As I sat on the Spanish Steps, the bustle of the tourists and the locals jump-started the entire trip.

The traffic puzzled me. How do the Italians survive the chaotic traffic? Motorcycles and scooters, taxis, busses, and cars dashed dangerously close. The streets sounded like an orchestra of noises with beeping horns and police whistles. The sound was deafening. The smell of gasoline and diesel fuel provoked nausea. No one seemed to know how to park their cars. The crowds pushed forward, with workers on bikes seemingly trying to smash tourists, in their haste to arrive at their destinations on time.

Fear became a factor in the Vatican. Our bus driver delivered forty of us to a special line to navigate through the Vatican. We arrived at 7:00 a.m. with the orange disk of sun rising on a hot October morning. The twenty minute wait in line gave us a big advantage, as many tourists waited several hours to enter. A local guide led us inside. We scurried along the halls like field mice.

We wore headsets to hear the guide, but I don't remember much. The ambient noise made it impossible to understand through the speakers. When we entered the Sistine Chapel, the wall-to-wall crowd prevented seeing much, except by looking upward at the most famous ceiling in the world. The travel books told about the time various painters labored throughout the years on the ceiling, adding to its splendor with the Botticelli angels and other scenes. I recognized Biblical stories on the ceiling, but I held onto Ed's shoulder with enough pressure to cause a big bruise. The word "claustrophobic" comes to mind. The bodies pressing so close together seemed to suffocate me. We made our way to the opposite door where I caught my breath and welcomed the fresh air.

Recently, the Vatican has made changes to prevent reactions such as mine. They installed new lighting and ventilation. If I visit Rome again, I will re-visit the Vatican, as I know my reaction prevented seeing the Chapel and the rest of the Vatican in its full glory.

The size of the plaza outside the Vatican astonished us. Television cannot project the massive structure, the details of the statues or crowds with the same reality we witnessed as we stood facing it. I pretended to see the Pope at the window. Little shops for tourists line part of the plaza. I managed to fit small souvenirs into the dark pockets of my overflowing backpack—a rosary for my Catholic friend and little medallions for others.

We sauntered along the main street of Rome, which was lined with retail shops offering leather, women's and men's shoes, fancy clothing, and cheap souvenirs. I managed to flee from Ed for a few minutes to purchase kooky, colorful knee socks for me, but nothing else.

Isn't Italy supposed to be the food capital of the world? I expected better meals considering the rave reviews I read in the travel literature. A typical dinner on the tour consisted of chicken, carrots, potatoes and amazing desserts. I pictured a similar meal on an Ohio menu, except for the desserts, such as real cannoli. On our next trip to Italy, I want pizza and dessert every night—or better tour food.

Our tour guide, about age thirty-five, handsome, multi-lingual, gave us a lecture about keeping up with the group when we arrived in Venice. With his jaunty cap and turquoise silk shirt with garish flowers, he looked Hawaiian, but hailed from California. He warned about pick-pockets and the dangers of becoming lost. We walked briskly to the speed boats which took us on the Grand Canal towards St. Peters' Square.

Murano, Italy, "street" or canal, near Venice

After a lecture by the owner of an art glass tourist trap near the Plaza, we marched to the gondolas lined along the pier. The gondoliers, dressed almost like pirates, lacked eye patches. They were mostly tall, strong, swarthy young men. We boarded the assigned gondolas with glee. I thought about packing one of the gondoliers in my suitcase as a souvenir. Someone at the front of the parade of gondolas winding through the canals of Venice sang recognizable songs, such as *"Volare"* and *"O, Solo Mio!"* The music bounced and echoed off the ancient buildings lining the canals. The gondola ride on a sunny, Italian day made up for all the disappointment of the food.

Ed and I grabbed a water taxi to Murano, after ditching the group. I loved the water-taxi ride, almost the same as taking a bus, but on water. We looked for the right pier for the route that carried townspeople, a few tourists, and university students to and from nearby islands. As I recall, the short voyage took about ten minutes from Venice to Murano. Looking out from the open-air boat, as Venice became smaller in the distance, gave us a different perspective of the architecture. The sounds of the sea gulls, the colorful speedboats, and fishing rigs added color to the adventure.

Murano is a mecca for glass-makers. As we crossed the water, we recognized the colorful Murano and Burano homes in the distance which we had seen during our travel research. The row houses glowed yellow, turquoise, or adobe in the bright sunlight. Glass factories and glass shops are abundant in Murano, which could be termed a suburb, if it were in the U.S. We found a small café for lunch situated beside a canal. We devoured our sandwiches and drank wine quickly at a tiny, round table in the shade outside the restaurant before racing through the little town to see the glass for sale.

The small independent shops for tourists held cheap trinkets and knock-off glass, probably from China. Since I collect paperweights, my disappointment became apparent as the paperweights in the fancy, retail shops of the glass manufacturers were overpriced for the quality. I found a small, crystal-clear glass paperweight in the trash next to a high-end, expensive retail shop. The weight, etched with a girl with a ponytail, showed no price tag. I took it inside, asking the clerk for the price. Sniffing with his nose in the air, as if he were a Frenchman, he let me purchase it for $5 U.S. dollars, "… as long as you don't tell anyone where you got it, Madame!" Their trash became one of my prize paperweights.

I fell in love with Morris (for *Maurizio*) and Max (for *Maximino*), two, elderly Italian guys on our tour, who lived in Las Vegas. Fun-loving brothers, who moved from Italy to New Jersey, as youngsters, they migrated to Vegas after both of their wives died a few years earlier. Morris told us proudly he turned eighty recently, while Max, the quieter of the two, shared his age as eighty-two. Many on the tour avoided the two old men because they cracked jokes like kindergartners and laughed too loudly for our conservative group. I enjoyed them. Max limped but willingly hobbled along with the group.

When we boarded the bus in Venice to return to the hotel for dinner, no Morris and Max. The bus left five minutes after the deadline. I worried about them, hoping they would appear at the hotel which seemed about twenty miles away. How could we leave them to fend for themselves? The guide commented indifferently, "They'll show up." I was furious.

As the group at the hotel started their dessert, the old geezers appeared in the dining room door. "Any food for a couple of old Italian guys?" asked Morris with a broad smile. We clapped and asked how our wayward, senior travelers found the path to the hotel. They didn't speak or understand Italian, but they walked into a place that said "*Polizia*" (Police) where they asked for a ride. Max found the phone number for the hotel in his pocket. The police loaded them on the right bus for the hotel.

I wandered to their table after I finished my cannoli to hear more details. They laughed and carried on. Yes, the police kindly reprimanded them. Yes, fear became a factor. I wondered if Max and Morris were the guide's grandparents or uncles who became disoriented or lost, how he would want them treated. My old buddies gave me a bottle of red wine they had purchased. Their disaster became a high point on their trip to share upon their return to Vegas. They turned their fear into bravado.

Onward to Florence via a trip in the bus around Lake Garda. Although the prices in Florence for retail tourists favored movie stars and wealthy politicians, we loved Florence. The churches look nothing like most large churches in the U.S. The carvings, the statues, and the paintings contribute to their architectural beauty. Our local tour guide led us to significant sites. At the entrance of the Palazzo Vecchio stands a copy of the statue of David. The original by Michael Angelo is kept at the Gallery of the Academy of Fine Arts to preserve it from weather and people. The history fascinated us. Given free time, we ate near the Palazzo. I wandered down the small alleys to find souvenirs. I considered expensive leather gloves, but opted for colorful scarves in various sizes, colors, and textures: paisley, plaid, flowered, garish, subdued and elegant. The enormous range of choices forced speedy decisions for gifts for special friends and family at home.

The trip officially ended in Florence, but we stayed another day to visit a few more sites before heading to the next step of our journey. Half way through this trip, we needed to wash clothes. We hand washed the shirts, hoping for successful drying in the open windows in our hotel room.

The Uffizi Museum remained high on my list of sites on

our extra day. We arrived before the crowds. Never have I viewed such a vast number of paintings of the "Last Supper" in one place. I wanted to see Michelangelo's *Doni Tondo*, painted about the same time that he created the statue of David. The masterpiece caused me to pause and breathe deeply. The depth and brilliant colors, the unusual poses of Mary, Joseph, and the Baby Jesus have lasted since the early 1500's. The magnitude of Christian art must restore faith for many who visit, despite the chaos of our crazy world.

In the afternoon I slipped out for a long walk while Ed napped. Our train trip to Milan and onward to Nice would leave early the next morning. As I walked across the Ponte Vecchio, a large, ancient bridge near our hotel, I thought about the history of the beautiful city and the art at the Uffizi Gallery. I knew little about Michelangelo's inventions, paintings, and music before our trip. I hummed a little tune of happiness.

Rain began to fall quietly. I scrambled to the hotel for my last supper in Florence.

Chapter 20

The Faux-Pas

In the morning, we began using our Eurorail tickets. Although I had studied the railway website and thought I knew the rules, I completed the start date on the ticket 10/9 (for October 9). Europeans write it backwards from Americans. The conductor between Florence and Milan spoke in loud Italian words mixed with superb English that I must get the ticket fixed in Milan. With little time between trains, I "fixed it" by writing in 9/10 for the ninth of October and scratched out the old number with a pen.

We saw nothing but the train station in Milan, since we had another train to catch within an hour. We ate standing at the counter in a scruffy, little cafe inside the terminal. There was no time to investigate the ticket. Growling stomachs won over ticket reparation.

"You must never do this again!" shouted the French conductor on the train from Milan to Nice. His voice resonated throughout the passenger car as if I had committed a bank robbery in a Casino in Monaco

"You must go to the train station to see if they can fix the ticket for you. This is illegal."

The conductor's voice rose in an unheard-of rage. Perhaps I would roast in hell for that error or minimally spend the rest of my life in a French jail in Nice.

Thoughts rattled through my head as the train traveled the tracks. *Was this a mistake not to fly to Lyon, rather than take a couple of days to see the sites on the way to Chambon? Maybe I should not have trashed the book about shopping in Italy to lighten my suitcase. Should we abort the pilgrimage to Chambon?*

The seven or eight hours on the train proved copacetic. Smooth, teal blue water with white cotton candy clouds rode with the train, starting not long after our departure from Milan. The Mediterranean sparkled on one side while the cliffs in hues of tan, brown, and dark blues became dipped in sunlight on the rocky bluffs later in the day. My head felt like the ball in a tennis match. With the adobe dwellings dangling precariously, the sailboats gliding through the tide, lapping at the beaches, no sleepy heads from America traveled in this train compartment. We created unforgettable memories with no regret of "wasting" the seven hours of bliss and relaxation with our heads bobbing back and forth along the Mediterranean shore.

The coach compartment offered uncomfortable seating with room for six fascinating people, including us, yet no one spoke. An old Asian couple boarded in Milan with a local guide or caretaker, hovering to assure her charges had their packages, suitcases, apparel and wits with them. The guide should have departed the train before it left Milan, but the train sped down the tracks with her rocking unsteadily on her feet. Commotion erupted when the same, disgruntled conductor discovered the guide. The old man gave the tall, skinny guide money for her return trip to Milan, when she left at the next stop. I wondered how the couple would manage at their destination. My bet is one of their suitcases weighed more than our two suitcases and backpacks added together. They clamored off the train in Monaco without speaking to or with us. I'm worried that they still may be wandering aimlessly around the town beside the tracks.

Since we arrived in Nice near dinner time, I avoided the inevitable trip to fix the ticket until the next day. Tired, but happy, we trudged to the exquisite boutique hotel I found online. Hotel Windsor brings fond memories to mind: small, elegant, and nicely furnished. The concierge established the ambiance with her recommendation for the evening meal at a nearby four-star restaurant. It was a splurge for such an expensive meal, but we needed it after the long train ride.

Nice is not only a technical, industrial city, but also a destination for tourists. Balmy weather, history, mountainous background, and beaches attract many nationalities. In the fifth largest city of France, visitors may enjoy museums or art galleries, while business associates dine in brasseries. I wish we could have spent more time in Nice, exploring the sites and shops.

After eating the best meal of the trip, we walked underneath the swaying palms beside the sandy Mediterranean beach. We watched the sunset change from bright Crayola colors to steel gray and tones of purple until the sun disappeared. The foothills of the Alps rose as a backdrop for a night of Heaven on Earth.

The croissant and coffee, served in the morning in the shade of the hotel garden, gave me the courage to face the attendant in the train station with my "illegal" ticket. After a forty-five minute wait, a large, female attendant called my number and looked at the ticket. With her teased hair, large bosom, and gigantic, red, pursed lips, she looked like the fat lady from a circus. She smelled of garlic, onions, and tobacco. Her large yellow teeth proved the years of cigarettes in her life.

I understood her *"Mon Dieu! C'est impossible!"* resounding throughout the room. A lengthy explanation allowed me to grasp I would need to explain my stupidity to each conductor along our merry path. The next conductor admonished me in an even louder voice, saying he could not take my ticket. Then he continued walking up the aisle collecting tickets from smarter people. Alarmed by his reaction, I figured *les gendarmes* or police would board the train to put me in jail, but it never happened.

After the brief encounter with the vociferous, hefty train station clerk, we trudged to the beach to find the spot for tickets to ride the little tourist "train" in Nice. The motorized vehicle circles the city streets in Nice, winding its way to the top of the cliffs. The phenomenal view from the top of the town assured me the train trip through the countryside made sense. Postcards from Nice don't lie. The Bay of Angels is appropriately named. Overlooking the dense city with the aqua-velvet, magnificent Mediterranean below created a view worthy of exclamation marks and many camera clicks.

With a little extra time before we caught the next train,

I convinced Ed to visit the flea market. Earrings, glass art, antiques, and everything imaginable attracted our attention in the open air market under the palms. I'm always amazed when Ed is so willing to look for "fleas." A pair of reasonably priced earrings slipped nicely into my purse. We made the best of a short stay.

I made a mental note that another trip to Nice would be nice. Our next stop would be Avignon.

Chapter 21

The Bridge in Avignon

Avignon made a dream come true. The first time I sang the little song about it in high school French class, I knew I wanted to see the bridge. Here I stood in the ultra-modern train station in Avignon. The soaring glass ceilings rise into an inverted V above the busy station. About twenty people disembarked, many with backpacks. The long, narrow waiting area looked like a cathedral without pews. Dusk surrounded us with its hazy blue and purple colors, glinting through the enormous windows. I wondered why no pipe organ played in the background.

I recall the walk from the train station to the hotel seemed far, as we dragged our suitcases along the cobblestones. Maybe the stones exacerbated the long walk. The unexpectedly large hotel room delighted me with its provincial colors: light blue and white printed cotton toile curtains with a white bedspread and a small bouquet of yellow chrysanthemums in a white vase. Dainty, yet functional.

As we rushed to dinner, Ed and I argued about where to eat, when really it didn't matter. We were hungry and tired, but realized the crowds were dwindling, and the restaurants were closing. Our raised voices softened after we gobbled our dinner.

The morning sun brought a spectacular view from our third-floor vantage. We could see people walking around the clock tower balcony and the brilliant red tile roof tops from our window. Flowers bloomed abundantly from window balconies and in cracks of the cement, with the landscaping below filled with brilliant colors. Breakfast included *les confitures* (jellies) for our croissants, fruit, and tasty, pungent cheeses. We left our hotel as the children's tune in my head spun repeatedly: "*Sur le pont, d'Avignon…*"

Off we strolled to *le Palais des Papes* (the Pope Palace), a monstrous edifice, constructed with the leadership of two Catholic popes: Benedict XII and Clement VI during the 1300s. The Gothic castle housed a total of six popes before returning the papacy to Rome.

This huge Gothic building remains as a reminder that six popes reigned in the palace. We observed the marked differences in the architecture with each section added. Each pope wanted recognition for his effect on the historic edifice. Monstrous stone work with ceilings higher than most cathedrals offers the opportunity to gaze and relive the history. Personal guides and hand-held audio devices regale stories of the past. The palace appeared dark and dreary with suggestions of ghosts in the corners. I wondered if the dank, chilly atmosphere inside the palace contributed to returning the papacy to Rome, as if Catholic leadership concurred that Rome offered a better location to unite more people in Christian Catholicism.

The Bridge in Avignon

The Bridge in Avignon

The sun warmed the day while global visitors ate, drank and relaxed in front of the palace; others roamed the gardens. The weather felt like spring, yet it was October.

The *Pont d'Avignon* (officially St. Bénezet Bridge) surprised me as it stops half way across the river. How did that happen? The bridge, constructed in the 11th century, began disintegrating in the 16th century from many floods. The bridge, mentioned in the song which children and beginning French students sing, needs a good structural engineer.

We had hit the high points. Walking the paths where the popes ruled achieved realism that postcards cannot project. Discovering the damage of the bridge caused ambivalence as I was disappointed to view the deterioration, yet elated to cross it off my bucket list. The distance to the train station shrank on our return walk over the cobblestones to the train.

The next legs of our adventure offered additional great expectations. The trip to Chambon from Avignon required a fast train to Lyon because no direct route to Chambon existed, unless we rented a car. In Lyon, we boarded a train to St. Étienne, where the train station stood directly across from our seedy hotel.

We arrived in St. Étienne late in the afternoon, taking a long walk before dinner. We noticed trash and dirt along the main street. At dinner, the waiter shared that St. Étienne is an industrial center rather than a tourist destination. After a few glasses of wine with our meal, we slept fitfully with the trains rumbling on the tracks across the street. Ed's snoring and my excitement kept me staring at the ceiling most of the night. We arose early to find the boarding area for the bus to Chambon.

Chapter 22

The Pilgrimage

The bus arrived promptly in St. Étienne to carry us to Chambon-sur-Lignon. The passengers talked in hushed tones, returning home after work or other activity in the industrial town of St. Étienne. I laughed as Ed's cell phone rang. His ring tone barked like a dog. Everyone on the bus turned to look at this odd man from America, wearing his white tennis shoes, while he struggled to silence "the dog" in his pocket. An hour from St. Étienne, we said good-bye to the jovial bus driver, who suggested we leave "the dog" in Chambon on our return trip.

In Chambon, I spoke only French but my ability to speak French had deteriorated with little opportunity to speak the language. "Òu se trouve L'hotel Bel Horizon," I asked the young man by the road. "Sign language" helped. We trudged along a small hill, dragging our suitcases along the pavement. The weather was overcast and gray, almost foreboding, as we reached the charming hotel.

The elegant French décor of the dining room, visible from the front door, coupled with the sweet smells of cooking, brightened the day. A huge bowl of mushrooms rested beside the door, ready for inclusion in a gourmet meal. The decorative touches reclaimed the elegance of a past era. We told him we wanted to eat dinner in the renovated dining room.

Colorful, dainty, straw flowers stood on each dining table in little glass vases. No pictures on the wall provided an updated, minimalist flavor, along with a few elegant antique pieces of furniture for an eclectic appeal. We noticed evidence of three or four children, probably in elementary school. We figured they lived at the other end of the hotel with the hotel manager and his wife. Bikes and boots appeared outside, but away from the main door, yet youngsters remained invisible.

A handsome man, around age forty, led us to our room, talking incessantly on his cell phone. The ceilings in our hotel room must have been twelve feet high, with gray walls, a fluffy white duvet and uncomfortable straight chairs. We heard no other guests, but it was early. After pulling my ugly, green rain jacket from the suitcase, we explored the surroundings. The sun brightened the day, but the wind whipped through the jacket.

I was stunned to see the *Maison de Repos*, otherwise called *Les Genêts*, across the street from our hotel. I had not noticed it on the trek from the bus. A small sign said *Rehabilitation*, the same word in both French and English. Had *Les Genêts* remained a rehab business all these years? Although I wanted to knock on the door to see the interior and visit the people, I huddled across the street. No one entered or arrived while I watched the door for a few minutes. I

Ruth by Les Genêts in 2006

failed to comprehend whether it was a rest home for senior citizens or people with infectious diseases or alcohol abuse. And I didn't ask. I felt my inquiry at the door would invade the patients' privacy.

Ed took photos of the building. The white shutters reminded me of the ones I had opened each morning in the summer of 1965. During my research I found that *Les Genêts* started as a non-profit 115 years ago, established by the Salvation Army to rehabilitate people.

A brisk fifteen-minute walk took us to the *Collège Cévenol*. I recognized the building where I audited the French-as-a Second-Language class. The campus seemed deserted except for one dormitory with young adults or teenagers, coming and going. A chill crept through my bones, not from the damp, cloudy day, but remembering more than I thought possible. The pine trees swayed in the strong breeze as I recalled the days when I crossed nearby fields for my classes. I wondered about the people I met long ago. What were they doing now? Would I meet Marie or her mother who both helped me find work that summer?

The town closed, except for the one small restaurant on the square or *centre ville* from noon to 3:00 p.m. We ate at the little restaurant while teenagers visited and ate their sack lunches across the street. I ordered *un croc*, a delicious ham and cheese sandwich, dipped and fried. Don't we call that delicacy a "Monte Christo" in the U.S.?

Continuing our exploration in Chambon, we walked past the Catholic Church and onward to the Reformed Church, which evolved from the Huguenot faith. Emblazoned, as I remembered, on the Reformed Church was *Aimez-vous, les uns, les autres* or "Love One Another" from the Bible (Luke 10:27). Quite a reminder, for all who visit, that the world would be a better place if we all loved each other. A reminder to us about the Nazis and the Trocmés. A reminder that we must never accept man's inhumanity again. The people of Chambon do not talk about their heroism during the war. Why not? Don't they want the world to know how they saved the Jews and others who needed protection? When asked, they look toward their shoes, saying, "We did God's bidding. We are not heroes. We did what was expected through faith and family."

Soon the stores re-opened, including the Tourist Office, which reminded me of my home town's Chamber of

Commerce. Children and teenagers filled the small office. They arrived for a casting call for an upcoming promotional film with the President of France who would soon visit Chambon. I visited with a lady in the Tourist Office, who said she would arrange a personalized tour for us the next day. She informed me that Chambon-sur-Lignon's population has remained about three thousand inhabitants in the past sixty years; however, as many as twenty-thousand French people invade the little town during August for their vacations. Not many foreigners come to Chambon, but children who attend the *Collège Cévenol* continue to arrive from current countries being ravaged by war. When we visited, they expected Albanians from Kosovo, suffering from the chaos of that war. The day passed quickly, as we walked around the small town, contemplating the new architecture which blended with the tall trees and countryside.

The cook at our hotel supplied us gourmet pleasure with the tastes and smells of the area. The mushrooms, previously in a basket by the entry, became part of the evening meal as a delicate mushroom soup. Five other tables of couples shared the meal. They seemed like locals, as they all spoke French in low tones; we listened to the lilting laughter of long-time friendships.

From my notes I wrote on this vacation, the meal included, "...mushroom soup, leeks, a fish roll which may have a little lobster in it, wrapped in what might be Canadian bacon. Then cheese and an ice cream roll slice. The Loire wine, also excellent." The gastronomic gift from the chef and sommelier pleased our tired bones. Memories bring back the pungent smells, the warmth of the people

The Huguenot Cross

we met, and the sounds of the children after school at the background.

We relaxed much of the next morning, Ed reading and talking too much, while I wrote a few postcards. We wandered down the road to the jewelry store on the square to buy two silver Huguenot crosses to carry home. One cross was a gift for the Presbyterian minister, who gave me resources into the catastrophic Christian history in this little town. The other cross was a gift for a favorite friend in Texas. I wear the gold Huguenot cross regularly, given to me when I worked at *Les Genêts.*

The Huguenot cross is rife with symbolism which one of the residents at *Les Genêts* explained to me long ago. The four "arms" of the cross represent the Gospels of Matthew, Mark, Luke and John in the Bible. Eight tips on the four arms symbolize the Beatitudes. Rounded edges on my cross epitomize the twelve Disciples. Four tiny hearts near the center represent loyalty. I love the little, dangling dove which represents *Saint Esprit* or the Holy Spirit, reminding me of the Trinity of Father, Son and Holy Spirit. I know it stands for desire for peace in the world.

After lunch, *Mme Annick Flaud* (pronounced Flow) arrived at the Tourist Office to lead us to a display of photos from the 1940's, housed in the former train station, a makeshift museum. When I recognized the picture of the little train which brought me to Chambon, I realized that train transported children sent to Chambon. I deeply regret not understanding the bravery of the people I met during the summer I lived in Chambon. I wish I had heard more of their stories.

Mme Flaud walked slowly, showing beauty from her younger days. She was outgoing, friendly, and fearless. Her grace and style at more than eighty years old set us at ease. This short, stout "tiger lady" with clipped, dyed red hair, wore a nose piece for her oxygen tank which she carried with her. Her maroon, slightly unzipped sweatshirt over a colorful silk, flowered blouse showed an ongoing interest in fashion when she met us at the Tourist Office for the brief walk to the museum.

Her historical presentation took place inside the old train depot, not much larger than an American living room. As she walked from poster to poster hung on beige walls, the story of Chambon came to life. The posters from World

Madame Flaud in front of a museum poster

War II showed pictures of the *Collège Cévenol* and the school children during the war, visually demonstrating diversity. The picture of the Jewish children playing in the snow during hard times brought tears to my eyes.

She shared that she'd survived Paris during the Resistance, moving to Chambon years after the war. When she saw no one telling the story, she volunteered. While the native *Chambonais* rarely talk about their experience, she bravely tells the story to foreigners who visit. Her presentation was a precious gift to Chambon, its visitors, and us.

Since we visited in 2006, a museum with more photos

and historical information opened in June 2013 across from the little Huguenot church. *Le Lieu de Memoire* or "Place of Memories" houses archives and offers space for events, recently donated relics, and photos from the Second World War, giving insight into the Resistance.

We returned to the hotel to rest and review the profound events of the day. Both of us wanted a small meal. I requested left-over mushroom soup, bread, and several glasses of the Loire wine. The evening flew with reminiscing and reacting to our personal experiences. Ed thought about his dad's lengthy time in Europe in the military while my mind wandered across the street to *Les Genêts*.

While at the Tourist office, I talked with the manager, who knew Marie returned to Chambon after her college days to teach at *Collège Cévenol*. I asked the outgoing lady at the Tourist Office if she would try to reach her. She left a message for Marie with my phone number. Marie never returned the call. I wanted to ask her questions about her history and her ancestors. I had to guess, like the other *Chambonais*, she may resist talking about the past. She remains a heroine to me.

The gift of her mother's phone number long ago changed my life significantly. I wanted her to know how her life impacted mine, taking me on a different path. If it weren't for that telephone number she gave me when she was an exchange student, I might never have known about Chambon. If I had not lost my suitcase, my life would not have been enriched with new people and extensive travel.

We arose at 4:30 a.m. to return by bus to St. Étienne for the train to Lyon and onward to Charles de Gaulle Airport near Paris. The weather remained misty and foggy, damp and dreary. A tiny, skinny, older lady in a raincoat, carrying a small suitcase, stood with us awaiting the bus. We chatted briefly. Her appointment with her ophthalmologist in St. Étienne created an opportunity to stay with her daughter overnight before re-boarding the bus to return to Chambon. I shared with her that I worked in Chambon and asked her if she knew Marie. She knew her mom, the lady who drove me to the *Maison de Repos/Les Genêts* for my summer job in Chambon.

As we boarded the bus, the little French lady quietly said to me, *Vous êtes un peu Chambonais*, which translates roughly, "You are a bit like the people of Chambon." I think that was my first realization why Ed insisted we make this pilgrimage. He saw the significance more readily than I did.

Since we visited in 2006, the school closed in 2014, after seventy-five years in existence. Former students and the townspeople hope another International School will purchase it with adequate money for marketing and revitalization.

On our last night in France we stayed in a formerly-lovely-but-worn-out hotel next to the train station in Lyon for the convenience of another early morning dash to catch the train. It was time to go to Charles de Gaulle Airport for the flight home. The deserted train station scared me. A toothless, homeless guy approached us for money. We pretended we spoke no French, which was not a very loving act.

The huge Charles DeGaulle airport was packed like a crowded box of crackers stirred with a stick. Armed guards, search dogs, armed militia, and wall-to-wall people kept us from boarding quickly. We almost missed our plane due to the chaos.

As we winged our way to reality, I said a prayer of thanksgiving for the role Chambon brought to my life and for its influence that remains with me today and hopefully in the future.

Part Four

Acceptance

Chapter 23

In Doc's Own Words

One small town in Central France affected my life in 1965. I knew about the six million Jews who died. Many books and articles detail facts of the 1940s, some boring and others fascinating. I wanted to talk with someone who lived in Europe at the time to hear personal accounts of the era.

My ninety-year-old cousin popped into my mind. I knew he studied in Europe, became a world renowned surgeon and settled in Florida before we met in person as adults. When the Internet developed, our friendship grew through the many anecdotes and political rants we exchanged. I called him to seek his perspective, because he had helped me plan our trip to Switzerland several years ago. He lived in Lausanne while he attended medical school in the mid-1940s. His experience reveals how heinous history can hide its ugliness.

In Doc's Words—

I attended medical school in the late 1940's in Switzerland. What a beautiful country! The war ended about the time I arrived. My ears burned with the multitude of opinions vs. facts about Swiss neutrality. I attended Université de Lausanne in Lausanne, a small city on Lake Geneva half way between the city of Geneva and Montreux for my medical training.

The small country of Switzerland is like an island with relatively no natural resources. With Germany, Lichtenstein, Italy, and France surrounding it, fear was justified during the war. Both Lichtenstein and Switzerland created plans to prevent caving to the Allies and Axis. Both countries wisely fortified themselves, geographically and politically, to remain independent.

The Swiss maintained a strong militia, led by General Henri Guisan, a former farmer with an astounding ability for excellent planning and training. His wise decisions about training a badly equipped army helped Switzerland survive. I thought it was brilliant their leadership stationed military personnel near the border to protect their country. Training the troops was a high priority. All Swiss served in the military from ages nineteen through sixty.

The Swiss Army mobilized in 48 hours when World War II started. They kept their uniforms at home with their guns, ready to go without hesitation or whining. Most could arrive at duty stations within an hour from their homes or businesses. They learned to climb in ice and snow while protecting each town with ammunition, food, and supplies. Willingly, their government spent money on training, despite the lack of equipment. I recall seeing a statistic that the U.S. had 100,000 military in

1939 while the Swiss mobilized 350,000 in the country of four million people.

Guisan created an interior "redoubt" or enclosed structures in the mountains where they stored their munitions. We couldn't see the hidden storage areas. The Swiss disguised much of their protection, always attending to the beauty of the country. A rose trellis and fences might prevent distinguishing the cannon behind it.

The Swiss cultivated parks to raise vegetables, realizing the desperate need for food. Those who made cheese trained to make fewer milk products and raise more grain before I arrived. They had a better and more complex system of rationing than the U.S.

The similarities to shortages in the U.S. were evident to me, as I was aware of rationing where I lived in California before coming to Europe. When I visited Geneva, American made cars seemed to be more abundant than in the U.S. We had had a severe shortage of gasoline during the war, which appeared to be no issue in Geneva.

I heard if a Swiss farmer owned a chicken, the chicken had to produce twelve eggs. The farmer would hear from officials with a financial penalty if he had naughty chickens.

The women wanted silk stockings. I asked my mother to send some. I was a bad-ass playboy when I lived in Switzerland. Those silk stockings helped me use my savvy ways with women. The ladies loved the stockings I could provide. I enjoyed the companionship. The women teased me about my Americanized version of French. Fond memories, for sure.

One Christmas my study buddies and I went to

Morocco. All of us had money and partied, bringing cigarettes back for the Germans. I wasn't the only guy who used cigarettes as money. Everyone smoked. Maybe not everyone, but the Germans, in particular, coveted my cigarettes. Our dorm room probably caused many of us to suffer from cancer years later, because you could smoke anywhere you pleased. But—back to the story.

Switzerland could have fallen in many directions. Inside Switzerland secret Nazi sympathizers and spies existed. The German Embassy housed many spies. I probably attended classes with them, as Lausanne had Germans, Swiss and French living in the same dormitories. Geneva played a pivotal role in maintaining sanity in a crazy world. Vigilant citizens in plain clothes or uniforms trained their eyes on their colleagues, friends and neighbors during the war, although as students, we rarely discussed our backgrounds.

Inadvertent air strikes happened over six thousand times. If they shot down a plane or came across a group of invaders, the Swiss captured them, imprisoning them in camps better than their home base camps. By the time I arrived, internment fences had begun to disappear. Most of the former prisoners had already traveled to their homelands.

American soldiers, shot down over Switzerland, did not fear internment. In fact, some may have ditched their bombers to get away from the fighting during the war. They often stayed in fancy hotels and played tennis when the weather agreed.

One of my friends in the dorm told a story about

meeting his long lost brother after the war. They determined they fought against each other before the war ended. I couldn't see much animosity—just relief that the war was over and everyone could love each other again.

I made a lifelong friend with one of my study partners. The professors lectured only. No books, only lectures. I studied French for two years in the U.S., thank goodness, plus I took one semester of German. Three of us, a German, a Frenchman and myself, would meet after class to check notes with each other to assure we understood. Becoming doctors created big challenges, translating and understanding the medical terminology. All three of us graduated with honors, but we struggled. Hans, the German, tall, thin, with blue eyes, tried to grow a blond mustache, but he wasn't the lady's man like I was. Although I'm short, I'm not chubby, even to this day. I exercised and walked everywhere. My personality seemed to attract the French and Swiss ladies, who enjoyed the gifts and entertainment I supplied. The German ladies—not as freewheeling as the others. Hans took my leftovers.

The French wanted to use Switzerland as a sanctuary for escape from the Nazi occupation during the war. Understandably, but sadly, they said only people whose "lives were in jeopardy" would be allowed to enter. They turned away children and others doomed to die in Nazi camps. Near the end of the war, I was told, Switzerland opened their borders to more people who wanted out of the occupied areas. I remember hearing the number of emigrants grew to over three hundred thousand.

Hans, my lifelong friend, and I often reminisced about

our experiences, as we enjoyed our good fortune in the friendship. I visited him many times all over the world after we both married and had children. He became a famous researcher, while I continued my studies in surgery, joining the military for my residency. He died a few years ago, and I miss him.

That university and my travels played an integral part of my life. I know doctors all over the world. My family has the best health care solutions. We've traveled extensively, learning something new at every stop, every time. I've returned to Switzerland repeatedly. Mostly we stayed close to Zermatt to be near the ski slopes. I can't travel much any longer, due to my age, but I can still hear the yodeling and polka music in my ears. My son and daughter started traveling with us when they were seven and five, growing up learning about the cultural differences and similarities of people all over the world.

I love Switzerland: the mountains, the valleys, skiing, the exquisite wine, cheese, and lakes. Although I've traveled the world, Switzerland remains an example for world peace with its ability to fortify, not flee from adversity. We would be wise to revisit their history in today's sorry world.

The discussion with Doc proved thought provoking. His studies began in Europe in 1947, the year after the war ended. Yet I heard no pathos for the devastation of the buildings shattered by bombs or the families separated by the war. Doc witnessed life returning to normal. People danced, smoked cigarettes, and milked their goats and cows. Maybe people in towns where they passed the crushed churches and homes daily remained more aware of the disruption in the world from the war than his experience.

I'm worried about the present world disruptions, but I heard what Doc said. We must travel the road to understanding others.

Chapter 24

The Phone Call

Although I love happy endings, I doubted Marie and I would re-connect. She's the exchange student who gave me her mom's phone number before I went to France. I planned to thank her for playing a role in my journey and to hear about her life. Sometimes endings are different from our hope and expectation.

As I approached the end of the first draft of the manuscript, I decided to try once again to call her. My research showed she returned to Chambon to work at the college. I found someone who attended *Collège Cévenol*, who verified her husband's name. My diligence paid off. I located an email address for her husband and her. She responded with an email to me which included her phone numbers. I failed to return the call as the manuscript needed more work. I wanted to be closer to finishing the book before I talked with her. I emailed her saying I would delay my call and why. No other contact happened for nine months.

With the second draft almost finished, it was time to call her. My ability to speak French dwindled over the years with no one in my life who speaks French. I worried. Maybe she would not want to talk with me. Maybe she was disabled. Maybe she had a horrible time when she lived in my hometown and would not want any contact with me. Maybe historical secrets kept her from wanting to talk with me. Worry and fear kept me immobilized. What if I could not reach her?

I continued researching her life. She had returned to Chambon-sur-Lignon after her year as an exchange student in my home town in Ohio. What would I discover about her? Should I try to call her again? Would she remember when she gave me her mother's number?

The irony with this fear makes me laugh. During presentations I give for unemployed people, I force the participants to repeat, "The phone is my friend." Yet job seekers continue to sit behind their computers, rather than raise the phone to the ear to call someone to help with the job search. I sat thinking about my silly fear in front of my own computer. I had a million excuses for not calling and would whine to myself that the manuscript still needed work. The marketing package remained unfinished. My phone service lacked international calling.

A former writing professor and his wife pushed me: "Just do it, Ruth!" I contacted my phone service to research the cost of activating "International calling." Since the cost was minimal, I activated it. I notified both her husband and her about my upcoming call. The day before my date to contact her, I tested the phone to assure international access functioned. Marie's French accent erupted in my ear, but as a recording. Still no confirmation. Timidly, I called the next

The Phone Call

day, but the same recorded voice mail message assailed me. On my third try, I left a "fractured French" message, saying I would call again the following week.

I had checked the time difference for the next call to occur in the evening in Chambon. My hands shook as I dialed the numbers.

"*Hallo*," she said. I didn't know whether to try my French or English. I had a list of questions, which went unasked. It didn't matter. Neither of us spoke well in our non-native tongues. We talked about fifteen minutes. I'm not sure she understood how grateful I was that we reconnected. To ask her if she remembered giving me her mom's phone number no longer mattered. I'm not sure she knew I visited Chambon in 2006, yet she and I talked like old friends, despite the effort in language comprehension. I asked her more personal questions rather than the ones on the printed questionnaire I had prepared. The questions are tucked in a file to yellow with age. Reconnecting with this sweet-natured person brought my story full circle.

Marie married a man from Chambon. They both worked at *Le Collège*, where I had studied in the afternoons after my duties at *Les Genêts*. They have two adult children and a grandchild. Her kindness radiated through the phone, although the communication lacked depth in understanding the other's words. I substituted French words for some English and Marie substituted English words for my inept French. We laughed and enjoyed the conversation. Her friendly demeanor eased my previous fears.

We discussed *Les Genêts* as I remained curious about its current status. The *retraite* is not a retreat, but a rest home for *les anciennes* or senior citizens. Her father spent the last five years of his life at *Les Genêts*. Her mother died before her dad. The building continues to house older people for physical therapy and retirement. Too bad I failed to knock on the door to walk through the halls and visit with the seniors when we stayed across the street.

Le Collège Cévenol sold to Chinese investors in 2014, much to the dismay of the townspeople and former students. Marie said the college houses a few international students studying the arts. The online documentation about the school calls for developing a sculpture garden and an international destination for tourists and students for cultural interchange. The investors and leadership intend to add classes for calligraphy, the Chinese language and eventually advanced cooking classes.

I think I heard Marie's nose snort as we talked about the new owners. Intuition tells me she and her husband miss the activity and students of the college. Although the conversation lasted only fifteen minutes, she responded positively to future conversation. I promised to send her a copy of the book which highlights the lessons learned resulting from her initial gift of her mom's phone number.

Chapter 25

Gift of the Bucket List

As I sit in my home office with its cheerful, robin's egg blue walls, I wonder what other gifts remain in my path. The walls surrounding me show a plethora about my life. The picture of the pink house where I grew up shocked me when I saw it. It had gray shingles when I lived there. The advertising poster of my dad's banjo band before I was born. A painting of bluebonnets that reminds me of spring after the icy winds of Texas winters. Best of all, the prints I purchased on my first trip to France recall the kindness of people I have met on my travels.

I want more pictures. I started a bucket list when my kids became adults, which keeps me packing and unpacking the luggage. Whether I travel to London, England, or Longview, Texas, people and relationships fascinate me.

I think about my naiveté when I first left my hometown for my visit to France. I remember the fun in Chambon, as Christine taught us to dance, but I learned more from the loss of the suitcase. Facing abrupt change forced me to tackle the real world. When I lost my "things," I discovered my strength.

As I gazed at the church on the top of the rock formation in Le Puy, I marveled at the startling workmanship begun in 962 A.D. *How in the world did it last into this century? How did they build such a magnificent edifice with no cranes and heavy equipment?* The adventure to Le Puy resounds with memories of the stories Monique shared as we rode through the countryside.

When I read about the Syrian crisis of immigrants living in tents in Calais, I picture the little Frenchman I met when on my return to search for my suitcase in Calais long ago.

As I reflect on my life, I wonder what happened to the fat lady in Nice and the coffee barman in Paris. I think about Max and Morris. Perhaps they are loafing in the casinos near their home in Las Vegas.

Gifts arrive in various shapes and sizes. The original gift of the suitcase enriched my life with conviction that remains in my heart. Today my suitcase holds my stories of travel where I continue to learn the history and culture of others. Confidence grows when role models appear in the path, reminders of the power of persistence and patience during change.

The words on the small church in Chambon echo when change erupts. "Love one another," etched in stone over the door helps heal pain from loss. Divorce, single parenting, remarriage, and other events interrupt expectations as my life evolves, giving me courage for change, making me stronger. Supportive friends and family help with difficult decisions and disruptions when no right answer seems

Over the door of Le Temple, "Love one another"

possible. Highs and lows, as steep as mountains and as deep as ravines, act as catalysts for fortuitous new beginnings.

I don't "let go" of people in my life easily. I want to know the endings. Often we dislike or don't understand loss and outcomes. Learning to accept hardship and happiness builds strong character. Understanding the differences in people leads to a more peaceful world. We take action when we can and we hope to reach acceptance.

Stories of the atrocities, which I heard from my new friends in Chambon, opened my eyes to the ruthless facts of the troubles they faced. I shake my head in disbelief when I realize the number of times religious persecution recurs. The stories of the children and adults saved by the people of

Chambon during the Holocaust brought new authenticity to my otherwise sheltered upbringing.

When a new loss occurs in my life, my adult children hate to hear one of my favorite sayings: "Things have a way of working out, not always the way we plan, but they do work out." And they do.

I continue to add places to visit on my bucket list, which I consider as gifts to maintain my momentum. Yesterday in a telephone conversation with my oldest granddaughter, age fourteen, I told her that I'm planning on a trip to New York City. Her response, "Grandma, you need to go to the Empire State Building. Be sure to take the ferry to Ellis Island and the Statue of Liberty. Are you going to a play? You gotta see *Wicked*. It was really great!"

My bet is she'll travel with her children as an adult. Her daddy plans annual trips for his family. In fact, all of my children love travel, even with the insanity of traveling long distances with their babies and children to visit us.

I'm excited about my upcoming trip. It's time to pack my suitcase again. I purchased a roll-around on sale which fits the current airline restrictions and I'm renewing my passport. It's time to move forward again.

Au revoir et bon voyage.